What People Are Saying About Habitat for Humanity...

"After serving as President of the United States, Rosalynn and I believed it was important for us to continue to make a meaningful contribution to people's lives. And we have, with Habitat for Humanity. We believe in Habitat's integrity, effectiveness, and tremendous vision. With Habitat, we build more than houses. We build families, communities, and hope."

Former U.S. President Jimmy Carter
—on the Carters' long-standing partnership with Habitat for Humanity

"No organization in America has done more to promote the cause of decent shelter for all people than Habitat for Humanity. But this vital organization is not only an energetic voice for housing as a human right; it is building more than twenty houses every day in more than forty nations. Under Millard Fuller's leadership, Habitat for Humanity has provided a vibrant testament to the power of love in action to those in need around the world."

Coretta Scott King, Founding President and CEO
The Martin Luther King, Jr., Center for Nonviolent Social Change

"Habitat for Humanity is an excellent example of Americans working together for the good of our nation. I commend the many volunteers who roll up their sleeves to build houses so that other families can have a decent place to live. Your generous efforts reflect the kind of commitment to volunteerism and service that is needed to change America for the better."

U.S. President Bill Clinton
—who worked with his family, and Al and Tipper Gore, on a Habitat house in Atlanta, GA

"Habitat is a program that has a lot of heart, rings a bell with our people, and fits in with the Dow corporate culture. This is a commitment from our hearts, not just our pocketbooks. We really see what can happen when people give time and energy to help someone else realize the dream of homeownership."

Kathleen Bader, Vice President
Fabricated Products Division, The Dow Chemical Company

"When I'm asked about housing success stories from our inner cities, the first group that comes to mind is Habitat for Humanity."

Jack Kemp
Former U.S. Secretary of Housing and Urban Development

"Habitat for Humanity has a program that succeeds in breaking the cycle of homelessness by providing new opportunities."

Kimberly Aiken
Miss America 1994

" . . . My mind has been renewed by the volunteers. For our families, you have made a big difference in our lives—a change we will never forget."

Mark Dorsey, Habitat homeowner
1993 Jimmy Carter Work Project, Canada

"A lot of people feel that they do volunteer work and that it doesn't have any impact—[but] those are houses—people are going to live there, and for many they're going to be the first homes they've ever owned. It's harder to have a bigger impact than that."

Tom Brokaw
NBC News anchor and volunteer at the 1994 Jimmy Carter Work Project

"It's impossible to tap the enthusiasm, the sense of civic responsibility and duty, and even religious zeal that comes with the Habitat workers. The truth is they touch lives in profound ways far beyond the bricks and mortar associated with building the houses."

Henry Cisneros
U.S. Secretary of Housing and Urban Development

"There is no way I could have ever bought with money any of the things I have learned or felt by working on this house."

Nancy Boyd
Volunteer, Bend, OR

"Habitat for Humanity International is one organization that would help us change the housing problems of the most needy people in our society. It is God's own project, I believe, which is why it cares for those people in our society who in the eyes of men are useless and hopeless. But, to God, they are precious and equal to the very important."

Uganda First Lady Janet Museveni

"Habitat for Humanity is building much more than houses. By building hope it is building relationships, strengthening communities, and nurturing families."

Paul Newman
Award-winning actor and Habitat supporter

"We thank and praise God for [our house]. I know this is God's house. He's just loaning it to us while we're here. I thank and praise God for the love of the people who want to help people in need."

Mary Mathis
Habitat homeowner

A Simple, Decent Place to Live

The Building Realization of Habitat for Humanity

A Simple, Decent Place to Live

*The Building Realization of
Habitat for Humanity*

Millard Fuller

Unless otherwise indicated, Scripture references are from the King James Version of
the Bible. Scripture references marked NKJV are from the New King James Version.
Copyright © 1979, 1980, 1982, Thomas Nelson, Inc., Publishers.

Library of Congress Cataloging-in-Publication Data
Fuller, Millard, 1935–
A simple, decent place to live: the building realization of Habitat for Humanity / by
Millard Fuller
p. cm.
Includes bibliographical references.
ISBN 0-8499-1196-6 (Hardcover)
ISBN 0-8499-3889-9 (Trade Paper)
1. Habitat for Humanity, Inc.–History. 2. Habitat for Humanity, International, Inc.
3. Housing. 4. Poor. I. Title.
HV97.H32F854 1995   95-4835
363.5'06'01–dc20   CIP
5 6 7 8 9 LBM 9 8 7 6 5 4 3 2 1

Printed in the United States of America

LOVE IN THE PLANS

Long days with glorious ends
Thank God for building friends

A potpourri of hopes and dreams
Blueprints. Plans and color schemes
Where to put the boards and beams
Giving love without end
Helping hands. Friendly grins

Faith in humanity is restored
With every nail in every board

Houses built on loving ground
Kindness. Caring it abounds

The unity is in the community
The hope is in our hands
We're all held together by
The love in the plans

Quite an astounding family
This "Habitat for Humanity."

—HEATHER LYNN COFFMAN
Habitat for Humanity homeowner
Gold Hill, Oregon

Introduction

Late in 1994 I received a phone call from my good friend Kip Jordon of Word Publishing in Dallas, Texas. He wanted me to write another book about the exploding growth of Habitat for Humanity. I told him I didn't want to write another book—not just yet. My fifth book, *The Theology of the Hammer*, had been published in May of 1994. I had worked on it for months and really wasn't interested in doing another one so soon.

Kip was insistent. His idea was to pull together some of the material from previous books—especially *No More Shacks!* written with Diane Scott and published by Word in 1986, and *The Excitement is Building*, written with my wife Linda and published in 1990—then update everything, add appropriate new developments and ideas, and get the book out in the Fall of 1995. He even proposed a title for the new book—*A Simple, Decent Place To Live.*

Kip said he could get writer Lynda Stephenson of Chicago to do the initial organizing of the material and writing of the first draft of a proposed manuscript. Lynda Stephenson had worked with Linda and me on *The Excitement is Building*, so we already knew what a talented writer she is.

Kip continued, "We've also got some marketing ideas on how to get this book into the hands of a lot of new people who need to know about the incredible thing that is happening with Habitat for Humanity."

"Okay," I responded. "When do you need a completed manuscript?"

"February."

"February!"

"All right—the end of March."

"That's a little better. I'll see what I can do."

So we were off. Lynda Stephenson did her work in December and January—and did it well—but much more remained to be done.

I recruited Jim Purks, senior writer at Habitat for Humanity International, to do research and editing work. He in turn recruited Paul Pegler, another dedicated staff person at Habitat for Humanity International. Both men had helped a great deal with *The Theology of the Hammer*.

In one long session with Jim Purks, I gave him a list of forty-three things to do in connection with the manuscript. He got Joe Matthews, our director of Communication Sevices, involved and Joe brought in staff writer Terri Franklin and graphic designer Debbie Nessamar. Terri helped edit the entire manuscript, making many excellent suggestions. Debbie coordinated production of the maps.

Marykate Wilson and Jane Emerson of our Development Department worked extensively on chapter 9 and Angela Foster in Communication Services helped locate the many photographs used throughout the book.

I did some limited work on the manuscript in February and early March. Then, I blocked off ten days in mid-March for concentrated writing and re-writing. Linda and I headed for the condominium of our good friends Joan and Kirby Godsey on St. Simons Island, just off the coast of Georgia. There, in ten fourteen-hour days—sometimes starting as early as 3:00 A.M.—I pulled everything together.

My wife and partner Linda worked right with me as she has done on every other book, word processing the manuscript time and again, making many valuable suggestions and providing plenty of support and encouragement. She also searched for and handpicked many of the photographs found in the photo sections. I am so grateful to her and to the persons named above for their dedicated and effective work on this book, which has truly been a team effort.

I also want to acknowledge and thank Joey Paul, Trade Division vice president at Word Publishing, for his help and encouragement, and Alyse

Lounsberry, also of Word, who served as the book's editor. These folks did a great job and I am deeply grateful.

Some of the material in *A Simple, Decent Place to Live* has appeared in earlier books, but almost everything has been updated and much new material has been added. If this is your first exposure to Habitat for Humanity, the exciting story is in these pages. If you've read my other books, you'll enjoy the updates and I do believe you will find a lot of new stories and additional information which will excite you even more and make you more determined than ever to make sure that everybody in your town, in your state, in the country, and eventually, in the world, has a simple, decent place to live.

As with all my other books, all profits made by Habitat for Humanity in selling this book and all royalties will go to build more houses. So, buy more books and give them to all your friends! You will quickly see as you read this book that a lot has been done—but *so much more* remains to be done. Your help and active involvement are urgently needed.

I fervently hope that what follows will speak to both your head and your heart.

Millard Fuller
PRESIDENT AND FOUNDER
HABITAT FOR HUMANITY INTERNATIONAL

Contents

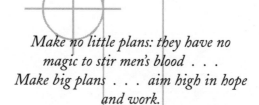

Make no little plans: they have no
magic to stir men's blood . . .
Make big plans . . . aim high in hope
and work.

—Daniel H. Burnham of Chicago
ARCHITECT AND PLANNER

CHAPTER ONE

Who Is Building All Those Houses and Why?

The Crazy Idea That Works

THE HOUSE COULD hardly even be called a shack. It was leaning precariously. It had no porch, the wood having long ago rotted away. Just a couple of cement blocks were being used as steps— up and into rooms which seemed nothing more than a collection of old boards still clinging to the few rusty nails that somehow managed to keep them upright.

Dim light revealed dirty clutter which was piled into the dark corners of the tiny house. Drapes over the window were nothing more than sun-worn rags, and where the windows were broken, other rags had been stuffed into the holes to keep out the night's cold. Nothing separated the hopelessly grimy kitchen area and the brown-stained toilet except a patch or two of the only pieces of decades-old linoleum still attached to the floor. Between the boards being passed off as a roof, leaves from an over-hanging tree had dropped through and were scattered here and there.

And outside, old tires, broken chairs, car carcasses, tall weeds, and trash covered the lot.

But on the lot beside it, down a short winding path, a small, simple house was being built.

The porch and the siding were already up and inside, young people and old, white people and black were grimy, tired, and grinning as they helped the new homeowner—the tenant of the shack next door—put the finishing touches on her new house. The new homeowner, a big barrel of a woman, eased down the narrow hallway to take another peek at her new bathroom with its actual porcelain tub before going back outside.

And as for the trash? "No trash is going to come anywhere near my house!" the new homeowner declared, swiping at an offending piece of muddy ancient newspaper as she stopped to admire for the hundredth time the blue siding of her dream-about-to-come-true.

From a patch of shacks in south Georgia to a South Dakota Indian Reservation . . . from a ghetto on the west side of Chicago to the sprawling housing areas of south Los Angeles . . . from the high Andes of Peru to the war-torn streets of Northern Ireland, this is a scene that's being repeated over and over again in all its variations.

Movie stars, Junior League members, sorority sisters, members of church youth and adult groups, civic club members, and professional football players have found they have at least one thing in common: They like to build houses.

So have Girl Scouts, nuns, college students, retirees, congressmen, and United States presidents.

Big corporations are forming teams to build houses. So are many associations.

The American Medical Students Association adopted this program in 1995. Scores of students from a dozen medical schools worked on houses in May and June of that year. The association has expressed its intent to do much more in coming years.

Doctors have built houses. A group in Louisiana called their effort "Physicians Making *House* Calls!"

Even lawyers have built houses—over five hundred attorneys took part in a unique indoor blitz build during the American Bar Association Convention in New Orleans. The completed house was then disassembled in sections and reassembled on a nearby lot. Building is happening everywhere . . . by everyone.

It is ecumenical. Catholics and Lutherans have worked side by side. So have Episcopalians, Pentecostals, Baptists, Mennonites, United Methodists, Disciples of Christ, United Church of Christ, and Presbyterians. All denominations and religious groups have built houses.

House-building is bipartisan. Gerald Ford and Jack Kemp agree with Bill Clinton and Al Gore about this work. Former President Jimmy Carter and wife, Rosalynn, have spent years giving their influence and carpentry skills to the cause. House Speaker Newt Gingrich wears a Habitat lapel pin. President Clinton mentioned Habitat in a State of the Union address. Jack Kemp, former Secretary of Housing and Urban Devolopment, has said, "When I'm asked about housing success stories from our inner cities, the first group that comes to mind is Habitat for Humanity."

(Photo by Gordon Peter)

Former President Jimmy Carter has been a strong supporter of Habitat for many years.

President Bill Clinton says Habitat is ". . . the most successful continuous community service project in the history of the United States. It has revolutionized the lives of thousands."

All this homebuilding has been the topic of conversation on "The Today Show" and "The David Letterman Show," the topic of articles in *Time, Reader's Digest,* and all of the major newspapers of the country as well as many of the hometown ones.

It has even been the subject of an episode of the television series, "Home Improvement."

But most of all, with the help of thousands of people like you and me, Habitat for Humanity has built houses—lots of houses. And because of all that building, families that had been forced by circumstance to live under bridges, in garages, tents, cars, shacks, and tenements are now living in simple, decent places and starting new lives.

These low-income families are able to afford their new places to live because the houses are modest, built largely by volunteers with the help of the recipient families, and sold on what we call the Bible finance plan: no profit, no interest, and a long-term repayment schedule. In short, the houses are not give-aways, but they are made affordable to needy families on very low incomes.

Believe it or not, by the end of 1993, Habitat for Humanity was the seventeenth largest homebuilder in the United States, according to a front-page article in *USA Today*.

I project that before the end of the decade Habitat will be the Number One homebuilder in the U.S.—in terms of the number of houses built. That will probably also make us the Number One homebuilder in the world.

We have reclaimed neighborhoods from drug dealers and squalor, and built houses that have withstood hurricanes, earthquakes, and floods. And the building just keeps on going.

Last count, over four hundred thousand people in more than twelve hundred U.S. towns and cities and in forty-three other countries had volunteered literally millions of hours to build houses. Over forty thousand houses had been completed as of late 1995, housing an estimated quarter of a million people! And new houses are going up at a rate of forty a day.

It took fifteen years to build the first ten thousand houses; the next ten thousand took two years; the following ten thousand came into being in just fourteen months; and the pace keeps accelerating.

Between twelve thousand and fourteen thousand houses went up in 1995. Plans for 1996—our twentieth year—include fifteen to seventeen thousand houses to be built. And in 1997 we should hit the milestone of twenty thousand houses to be built in a single year!

It's called Habitat for Humanity, and we build houses for *and with* those who need them.

Yes, it sounds crazy. On a vacant, littered lot in the midst of a decaying neighborhood, a group of volunteers in Portland, Maine were working on their first project—a duplex—when five carloads of out-of-state volunteers drove up. The first thing they saw as they turned off their engines was graffiti that had been scrawled across the half-built structure:

HABITAT FOR INSANITY

If insanity means doing things in unexpected, unusual, unorthodox ways, that's what this idea is—*insane*. Volunteers giving months, even years, of their lives. Supporters giving enormous chunks of their cash. High-salaried professional people giving their time and skills for free. Poor families giving their own "sweat equity." A former president and first lady of the United States donning work clothes and doing manual labor. And most surprising of all, no profit being made by anyone, because the homeowners are charged no interest. No question about it— to most people, the whole concept sounds crazy!

So why are we doing it?

People are always asking me the same questions about this crazy idea that works. So let me answer a few right now. I have never met a man who *liked* living in a house that leaked—have you? I have never met a woman who *liked* living in a house lacking enough insulation to keep warm—have you? Nor have I ever met a family who *liked* living in a house with holes in the floor or holes in the ceiling—have you? It is hard to break out of the cycle of poverty that has meant years of get-by living in a broken-down shack. Owning one's own house has been called *the American Dream*. But it's bigger than that. We're dealing with something that's universal in scope. The dream is not only universal; it is basic. And people everywhere understand its intrinsic truth:

Everyone who gets sleepy at night should have a simple, decent place to lay their heads.

Everyone needs a simple, decent place to live. And providing it is elemental goodness, truth, and love in action. To me, what we are doing is the very essence of true religion.

What then is Habitat for Humanity's goal? The answer is simple and outrageous. I first knew the answer to that question several years after Habitat was founded. I was being interviewed on a radio show in San Francisco in 1981 when a caller asked that question. No one had ever asked me that before. But from the depths of my soul, I immediately knew the answer.

"To eliminate poverty housing from the face of the earth," was what I told the caller—and I even surprised myself.

That's it, I thought. *That's our whole vision!* For years, we had focused on our own local area and on the country of Zaire, and we'd begun to see it happen in a few cities across the United States. Also, there was budding work in Guatemala and Uganda. But now the *Big Picture* had suddenly snapped into sharp focus. Our goal wasn't just to build a few thousand homes in Georgia or New Hampshire or Zaire, Uganda, or Guatemala.

Our goal was—and is today—to simply eliminate poverty housing from every state in the United States and from every country in the world.

The caller gasped on the other end of the phone line. So I continued, "And when we get rid of all poverty housing, we'll start on something else!"

She gasped again, and then gave a faint laugh. And immediately the station's phones started ringing off their hooks with people wanting to know how they could get involved.

The boldness of the goal stirs people, and each year we are amazed at what fresh miracles come from such boldness.

That moment even stirred my own heart again. Not too many years earlier, I had set myself a different goal: To become a millionaire as quickly as possible. Now my life had a new goal. *Could we be so bold as to think of building enough houses for a million people?*

Why not?

Why not even more?

Make no little plans, advised one of the century's most important architects.

Habitat's big, bold idea stirs hearts in the best possible way.

Local groups called affiliates are organized to build houses with and for needy families. New Habitat for Humanity affiliates are being added at the rate of ten to fifteen a month. These affiliates become officially connected with Habitat for Humanity International by signing and adhering to a covenant which embraces the basic principles of the work. (This covenant is included in Appendix One.)

Family selection committees review applications from people who are homeless or who live in substandard housing and who are unable to obtain conventional financing. As funding and land become available, families are chosen to receive Habitat houses.

Volunteers working with the chosen families build simple, decent homes of solid, quality construction. The houses are then sold with no profit added and no interest charged. Small monthly payments are made to repay the cost of the houses, usually over a period of ten to twenty years.

Neither race nor religion is used as a criterion in choosing the families.

Each affiliate is financed by a revolving Fund for Humanity made up of homeowners' monthly payments and donations raised from private sources such as individuals, churches, and corporations. Government funds are not accepted for the building of the houses, to ensure the grass-roots strength of the work and so that our ability to function as a Christian program is not compromised. City, county, state, and federal government help is solicited and gladly received for land, streets, sidewalks, etc. (setting the stage to build) and for some personnel and administrative expenses. The work done by the Habitat families is called "sweat equity," a concept that requires that they must work several hundred hours to help build their own houses and houses for others.

The whole concept is simple, and it works.

Paul Newman, Amy Grant, Jack Kemp, Jimmy and Rosalynn Carter, Bill and Hillary Clinton, Tom Brokaw, Jane Fonda, Al and Tipper Gore, 1994 Miss America Kimberly Aiken, Bob Hope, Newt Gingrich, Reba McEntire, and people like you and me—these are typical Habitat volunteers.

That's who have helped build houses. Whether through sponsorship, donations, media exposure, or hammering nails, volunteers like these are doing the job.

Jimmy Carter said it well in a *House & Garden* magazine article:

"Our volunteers are college students, former Peace Corps workers, retired clergy and business leaders, teachers and professors on sabbatical, and a cross section of Americans who are eager to devote their vacation weeks to building homes in this country and abroad. We work side by side with members of the homeowner families, sawing lumber, making bricks, Spanish tile, and concrete blocks, digging and pouring foundations, erecting stud walls, constructing roof trusses, repairing dilapidated parts of older buildings, and putting the finishing touches on the new houses and apartments. Our projects are not based on charity, and we do not assume the roles of generous and somewhat superior benefactors but of real partners with those who will occupy the new homes."

It works because the crazy idea is tangible. While so many of the world's needs increasingly seem to be too overwhelming for a single person or group to make a difference, building a simple house for one family in need *is* possible and, therefore, exciting. You can swing a hammer, pound a nail, hang drywall, install kitchen cabinets; you can work alongside a homeowner and share the joy. And afterward, you can take a picture of the houses. It has been said that people will support *anything they can take a picture of!*

You can hear how people who have lived in squalor, with overgrown yards, amid junk cars and unrelenting hopelessness vow not to let a piece of trash on their new property and experience the dawn of human dignity as it is born within them. The transformation is real and instantly recognizable.

A simple, decent place to live can break this vicious cycle of poverty and hopelessness. I've seen it happen over and over again. The effect that a simple, decent place to live has on these families is dramatic— especially for the children. Hope, pride, gratefulness—you can make a difference and be there to see it happen.

Habitat for Humanity works because it enables people to put their faith into practice. It is an acting out or, literally, a building up of what many people believe to be God's will and way.

It works because it's a hand up, not a handout. It's empowerment on the most basic level. Each homeowner family is expected to help build

(Photo by Julie Lopez)

Habitat for Humanity is replacing shacks with simple, decent places to live.

their own house and others. The mortgage payments on the no-interest, no-profit loans go back into a fund to build more houses. The result is lower housing costs, pride in ownership, and positive relationships.

It works because it is just common sense.

Everyone who gets sleepy at night ought to have a decent place to sleep, on terms they can afford to pay.

No matter whom I talk to, be they rich or poor, all people can agree on that truth. It's one of those rare things you can say that will elicit almost universal acceptance.

I have always felt that a house is to a human family what soil is to a plant. We all seem to know this deep down. You can pull a plant up out of the soil, pour all the water in the world on it, give it plenty of sunlight, and it will eventually die because it is not rooted. A plant needs to be rooted. A family is like that. If a family is not rooted, it will not flourish. It will not grow . . . will not blossom. But once a family is well-rooted, all kinds of wonderful things will begin to happen.

Soon after the family moved in, I talked to the man who owns the 30,000th house Habitat built. "The house is wonderful," he told me. "I'll tell you what—it's hard for me to be at work. I just want to be at home sitting in my house. I hate to leave and as soon as I get to work,

I can't wait for work to be over because I'm going to go home and be in my house."

The same thing happens with children. Their self-image improves overnight. They begin to do better in school because they have a decent place to study. We typically see this dramatic transformation. Children become better students with fewer behavior problems after they have been provided a simple, decent place to live. What Habitat does is much more than just sheltering people. It's what it does for people *on the inside*. It's that intangible quality of *hope*. Many people without decent housing consider themselves life's losers. This is the first victory they may have ever had. And it changes them. We see Habitat homeowners go back to school and get their GEDs, enter college, do all kinds of things they never believed they could do before they moved into their houses. By their own initiative, through their own pride and hope, they change. Three children of the first family to occupy such a house studied hard there—and became a lawyer, a psychologist, and a nurse. And the child of one of the most recent families—a family that had previously lived in a garage—is now making straight A's.

There are countless stories of people just like these who have become productive members of society after moving into their simple, decent Habitat houses.

We are all connected. Who doesn't want their community to flourish? And as long as there are shacks in any community, the community is less than well. A Habitat home can be the first step to bringing those who've been left behind into the fullness of community life. The community is always the better for it—we know that by experience.

Habitat for Humanity works because of its own bold vision. No more shacks! No more homeless people. Everybody laying down to sleep at night in—at the very least—a modest, good, solid house, on terms they can afford to pay. Habitat works because it is worldwide. Each local Habitat affiliate is expected to give 10 percent of its contributions to build in under-developed countries as they are building locally. Millions of dollars given through Habitat's tithe program, supplemented with direct contributions given by individuals, churches, corporations, and other groups in the United States and other countries make it possible to build ever-increasing thousands of houses for some of the world's poorest people.

Is it possible for everyone to have a simple, decent place to live in our world? The vision of Habitat says, "Yes." We've seen the miracles that come with this simple belief coupled with the simple action of making it happen—one family at a time.

People find the road to Habitat for Humanity in many ways, for many reasons. But the more volunteers and potential homeowners find their way to a Habitat building site, the more they are part of the solution.

What solution? There are many solutions—all of them good, all of them gratifying and uplifting for all concerned. This may be the best win/win deal in the world today.

I'd like to tell you the story of the beginning of Habitat for Humanity. You may already know parts of it or perhaps you have never heard any of the story. I do hope it stirs your heart.

CHAPTER TWO

How Did It All Begin?

The Personal Story Behind Habitat for Humanity

I N A WAY, MY OWN ROAD to Habitat started in a New York City taxicab. My wife Linda had just left me. It had been the shock of my life. After all, we were *millionaires!* We had a fancy house in a nice part of town with a Lincoln Continental in the driveway, a maid to clean the house and take care of our two children, two power boats, a cabin on a lovely lake, a huge farm stocked with cattle and horses, fishing lakes, and a big bank account. Wasn't that the American Dream? Wasn't that the very essence of success—the ultimate fulfillment in life? I had certainly worked diligently for several years to achieve it.

"No," she had told me. No.

It had taken me a while to understand. There in that taxi with her, trying to save our marriage, I suggested something that has made all the difference. "Let's give all this stuff and the money away," I said. And I saw a glimmer of hope in her eyes.

That was a startling, seemingly impossible idea for someone like me. My whole life had been geared to making money—as fast and as furious as I could. I was an all-American, Alabama church-going boy. But I was ambitious; I wanted to make something of my life. And I knew the way to do it was to make money and lots of it—to be successful in the classic sense of the word. Wasn't that the American way? After all, I seemed to have a gift for making the American Dream happen.

When I was growing up, our family lived in the small east Alabama cotton mill town of Lanett, where my father owned a grocery store and a drive-in short order business. I often helped out in the store and drive-in, but, as early as age six, I had my own little businesses going too. My first business was raising pigs and keeping my own record book of the profits. By my teenage years, I was raising rabbits and chickens and trafficking in used automobiles. I even got into selling firecrackers. My dad and I also had a cattle partnership on a farm he owned out from town. Business on the side was part of my life all through Auburn University, although my activities during college were a little more sub-dued. But then, when I entered law school at the University of Alabama on a whim because I liked politics, I met a fellow student who thought big—just like me. We were student-tycoons, thinking up any and every idea we could to make money.

We sold pine cones, corn stalks, and Christmas trees. We chopped down chinaberry limbs, painted the berries silver, and sold them as "Oriental berries." We sold advertising for desk blotters and a student telephone directory. We developed a birthday cake service by mailing a letter to students' parents right before the students' birthdays, offering to deliver their dearest college student a cake on the important day. It worked; all the ideas worked. Well, almost all of them. We tried pre-selling mistletoe to florists, but couldn't fill the orders because we hadn't figured on the mistletoe growing so high up in the trees and being so hard to cut down. Plus, selling mistletoe by the pound wasn't exactly smart, since we hadn't figured on how light the stuff was when we finally did get it down.

Still, we were full of ideas.

We sold trash can holders and doormats and holly wreaths by mail through clubs like the YMCA and made so much money, we invested in real estate. We started by renovating an old house. Then we bought a vacant lot and put mobile homes on it to rent to students; we bought another vacant lot and put an old army barrack on it and rented that out. By the time we were seniors, we were renting out half a city block to students. As we approached graduation day, we were already making more money than most people would make many years later.

Upon graduation, we opened a law office in the capital city of Montgomery and were lawyers by day and entrepreneurs by night. We sold tractor cushions through Future Farmers of America and gave away tractors as prizes. We sold twenty train carloads of tractor cushions in the first three months and with the money, bought a house which we converted to an office. Our next big project was selling cookbooks to Future Homemakers of America—a logical move from Future Farmers, we thought—the first one being *Favorite Recipes of America's Home Economics Teachers—Meats Edition.* Before we knew it, we were a huge publisher of cookbooks and moved on to every women's group we could imagine with the idea. We even sold a cookbook that contained only blank pages. *My Favorite Recipes,* we called it. Each woman could write in her own favorite recipes. It sold thousands of copies! After two years, our businesses were growing by such leaps and bounds, we had to close the law office for lack of time to devote to it.

We outgrew the business office so the back was knocked out and the size increased by 50 percent. We soon outgrew that. A much bigger building was purchased from an insurance company. That was outgrown, the back knocked out, and the building expanded. We outgrew that. A separate building was put up out back.

We got into selling candy, toothbrushes, and publishing many other books in addition to the ever-growing assortment of cookbooks.

And with all that income, I bought a choice twenty-acre lot and drew up plans for a bigger house. My partner and I purchased more farm land, and horses to ride on the land, and cars paid for with cash, and boats—all the things I had always thought would make me and my young family happy.

From the very beginning of our business partnership, my partner and I shared one overriding purpose: *To make a pile of money.* We were not particular about how we did it; we just wanted to be independently rich. During the eight years we were partners, we never wavered from that resolve, working from breakfast meetings to midnight brainstorming sessions. So when the company treasurer marched into my office one day in 1964 to announce that I was worth a million dollars, I wasn't surprised. I started immediately thinking ahead.

"What's your next goal?" she asked.

"Why, ten million," I answered. "Why not?"

There was a price, though. First, it began to show in a slipping of my own personal integrity that I hardly noticed. I remember at the university, when we'd need lumber for repairs on our rental properties, we would go to the buildings and grounds supervisor and get permission to take a few pieces of old lumber. When he left and no one was looking, we would take all we needed—new and used alike. As the years went by, we were always honest with our customers—that was good business. But as for our suppliers, a fair deal was never the point; making the *best* deal for our company was.

Next, the price began to show in my health: neck pains, back pains, kidney problems, a sore on my ankle that wouldn't heal, even episodes of not being able to breathe. Hundreds of times I had to grab the arms of my chair and struggle to fill my lungs before I could relax enough to breathe normally.

Foremost, it began to show in my marriage. I'm an ardent believer in American free enterprise. But it's like dessert; if you eat too much, you get sick. And by age twenty-nine, I was getting sick. I am the kind of person who is totally consumed, totally focused; I had no concept of balance, and I certainly couldn't see past my lifelong goal. Linda, though, saw what I could not see—that our marriage also was sick from my incessant drive to make money.

But I ignored all the signs and pushed ahead toward making the next million . . . until the day Linda walked into my office and announced to me that she didn't love me any more.

I was astounded, thinking: *I bought you a Lincoln. I bought you two thousand acres of land, two speed boats, a cabin on the lake. I am paying for your college education; I got you a maid. You have so many clothes you can't get them in the closet! I've done everything for you! How could you not love me?* But before I could say anything, she was speaking again.

She told me that what I wasn't giving her was myself. She said she never saw me. She complained that the business was taking all of me.

I promised to spend more time with her and the kids. I meant it; Linda wanted to believe it too. And the matter calmed down, or so I thought.

But a year passed and nothing had really changed. I still was putting in the daybreak-to-midnight hours.

So one day, Linda told me she was leaving. She said she was considering a divorce and needed some time to think. Because she didn't want to air our dirty laundry in town, she'd decided to seek counseling from a pastor she knew in New York City.

I could not believe it! To find out that I couldn't buy love was a startling revelation. Ever since I was a teenager, I had always been in control of things. Whatever I was involved in, I was the head of it. Whether it was running a Junior Achievement company, managing a little business, or heading up the youth program of my church, I was in charge: *my* company, *my* project, *my* group. I always knew what was going to happen, and I *made* things happen. It was the biggest shock of my life to realize that a decision was going to be made about our marriage—and it wasn't going to be made by *me*.

Linda and I were married when I was a senior in law school, and I loved her dearly. As I was growing up I always dreamed of having a loving family. My mother had died when I was very young, and I didn't get along with my stepmother. She was a fine woman, but we just clashed. I always wanted a family where there would be a lot of love in the home. Now, when I thought I was showing my love the best way possible, I was being told I had miscalculated tragically.

Linda left.

The long week that followed was the loneliest, most agonizing week of my life. At five o'clock each afternoon, instead of the usual midnight, I went home. Our maid needed to be relieved of keeping the kids. I took Chris and Kim for walks, played with them, and tucked them into bed. One evening as I was pulling the blanket over my son, he looked up at me and said, "Daddy, I'm glad you're home."

A chill traveled down my spine as I realized that Linda was right. I had indeed become a virtual stranger in my own house.

By the weekend, I knew I couldn't sit at home by myself. So I arranged for my folks to keep the children, called a pilot in our company, and said, "Get us a plane. I want to take a trip."

"Where do you want to go?"

"Let's go to Niagara Falls."

"Niagara Falls? Why Niagara Falls?"

I didn't have much of an answer. *Why Niagara Falls?* "Because I've never seen it," I said, my crumbling marriage on my mind. "I just want to go up there and see it."

So we rented a plane and flew to Niagara Falls—almost crashing for the effort. Ice built up on the wings as we were descending. We also lost touch with the control tower and nearly hit a commercial aircraft. November at Niagara Falls was not like November in Alabama! I hadn't thought about that. The story could have ended there, but it didn't. I had wanted to come to Niagara Falls, and there I was. *Now what?*

We rented a hotel room on the Canadian side of the border. I turned on the television. There was nothing else to do until I could talk to Linda. So watching an old movie was how I spent that night there in the middle of my marital crisis at Niagara Falls—confused, dazed, and numb. But a line from the movie leapt out at me, as if it had been written just for me. Hearing it was like a jolt to my heart:

"A planned life can only be endured."

That's what I was doing—enduring life. My plan was to get richer and richer, until finally I'd be buried in the rich section of the Montgomery Cemetery. And right then, by all indications, I was headed there.

I picked up the phone. I knew I had to talk to Linda. Finally, she agreed to see me, and my pilot and I were back in the air—this time headed for La Guardia Airport. I never told him why. I just said, "Leave me here and go back to Alabama. I'll get myself home."

So I went to New York to see Linda. She was staying at a Manhattan hotel. I arrived—nervous but determined. As we talked, we decided to go to Radio City Music Hall. The Rockettes performed. Then came the movie: *Never Too Late.* That made me smile, suggesting hope. Standing in the refreshment lounge during intermission, Linda began to sob. We left the theater and began walking, stopping to sit for a while on the steps of St. Patrick's Cathedral, then walking again. Somewhere off Fifth Avenue, we opened up to each other. Linda spilled out all the hurt and the secrets that had built up as our lives had grown apart. She cried as I had never seen her cry before. I cried. We held each other. Reconciliation commenced. Love began to be reborn.

The pastor had told Linda she could love me again if she had ever loved me. She held to that thought and said she was determined to try. I certainly wanted our marriage to work. I loved Linda so very much. I loved our little son and daughter. I desperately wanted us to stay together as a family.

A light rain began to fall.

We hailed a taxi. *The* taxi. As it rolled along the wet streets, there was a sensation of light in that taxicab. It wasn't anything spooky. Perhaps it came from the conviction I felt concerning what I was about to say, but I turned to Linda and told her I felt we should totally change our lives. We should make ourselves poor again, give all our money away, and start over.

"What do you think?" I asked.

I saw that glimmer of hope in her eyes, and I knew she agreed.

Later that evening we called the pastor who had been counseling Linda. His reaction was one of surprise. He was glad about our budding reconciliation but cautioned us about making such a radical decision so quickly.

"Wait until the morning. Think it over," he suggested. "And come see me."

But we had decided.

The following morning, we hailed another taxi, this one in front of our hotel, and the first one we saw stopped to pick us up . . . a miracle in itself! We climbed in.

"Congratulations," said the cabby. "This is a brand-new taxi. Nobody has ever ridden in it." This time, we both laughed and cried. We felt that God was confirming us in our radical, crazy decision. A shiny new taxicab . . . a fresh start . . . how exciting!

What do people do after making such a decision?

Our first priority was to get our family back together, so we spent two weeks just driving through Florida, enjoying being with the children and each other. On our way home, though, I began to seriously wonder what the next step should be. We stopped for breakfast in Albany, Georgia. I thought of a man named Al Henry who'd moved to a place called Koinonia Farm somewhere near Albany after he'd been thrown out of a Birmingham church for preaching integration. He had invited me to come for a visit, but I had no interest in going. In fact, I'd felt sorry for him at the time. Old Al had battled the forces of evil and lost—and then gone into the wilderness never to be heard from again.

But on a whim in Georgia that day, I decided I'd accept that old invitation. Next thing my family knew, we were driving forty miles north to a town called Americus to visit Al and to check out this place called Koinonia Farm. Al introduced me to Clarence Jordan, Koinonia's founder. Here was someone who not only liked the decision we'd made but thought it was logical. I wanted to talk more to this man. We'd planned to spend two hours there; instead, we spent a month.

Clarence Jordan was a radical himself—a radical Christian, a pioneer in many ways, a humble scholar with a doctoral degree in Greek New Testament and a well-known speaker and writer who was best known for his "Cotton Patch" translations of the New Testament. In his "Cotton Patch Gospel," Jesus was born in Georgia, where there were whites and blacks instead of Jews and Samaritans. (Years later, a Broadway musical, *The Cotton Patch Gospel* based on Clarence Jordan's Cotton Patch translations was produced and performed not only in New York but all over the country.) His community was integrated in the '40s, open to everyone, totally committed to non-violence and economic sharing—in other words, a Christian community, ahead of its time in racial matters which was radical enough in itself. But he was *beyond* his time with his idea of communal sharing patterned after the first Christians. More than once he was reminded that they existed in the middle of the cold war against Communism, in a time when economic sharing sounded a little "un-American" to many people.

At first, they sustained themselves by raising farm products. They sold to local people as well as tourists at a roadside market alongside U.S. Highway 19, a principal tourist route for people traveling to and from Florida. But then in the late '50s, the Ku Klux Klan and other segregationists turned against Koinonia because of its stand on integration. The roadside market was burned, rebuilt, bombed, then abandoned. Night riders began to shoot into Koinonia houses. Local citizens harassed them out of fear and suspicion, and a total boycott was imposed on the farm. So Clarence and those at the community created a pecan and candy mail-order business, and with his sense of humor firmly in place, coined the mail-order slogan for the little business: "Help us ship the nuts out of Georgia!"

By the time we visited Koinonia, it had dwindled to a small community, but its impact on our family was tremendous. While there, my partner joined us and we made plans for him to buy my share of the business and to help me give my money away to designated charities over consecutive years until it was gone. After a month at Koinonia, we left. But in two years, we were back, ready for a new direction.

(Habitat for Humanity file photo)

The Fuller family at Koinonia Farm.

During those two years as I continued looking for direction, I first took a fund-raising position in New York City with a small African-American United Church of Christ-related school— Tougaloo College near Jackson, Mississippi. Our family moved into an apartment located over a garage in New Jersey.

Of course, even during my business years, I hadn't given up my church involvement; I still believed in Christ as I did when I was head of my church's youth fellowship for the southeast region of the United States. And besides, in many sections of the country, particularly the South where we lived, being an upstanding member of the church was good for business. I even took on some regional responsibility in our denomination, the United Church of Christ. During that time, I'd been offered a chance to visit Africa to see how the church's missionary work was doing and to speak about what I saw on my return, but I declined because being gone from my business that long would cost me too much money. The sad part was that I had wanted to go, had even felt led to go, but I had told myself I'd think again about it in two years . . . maybe.

Well, a lot had happened in those two years, but when I was offered the chance to go again six months after that taxi ride in New York, I took a two-month leave of absence from my new job, and Linda and I went to Africa. A year and a half later I wrote Clarence Jordan. Koinonia had never been far from my mind. I asked him what he had up his sleeve.

He replied, "Millard, I don't have anything up my sleeve, but perhaps God has something up His sleeve for both of us." So Linda and I headed for Koinonia, and our lives found a new path. The forerunner of Habitat for Humanity was about to be born.

It was now 1968. At Clarence's invitation, we became deeply involved with a plan called Koinonia Partners—especially a vital part of the new work called Partnership Housing.

We would lay out forty-two half-acre sites on the north side of Koinonia's large farm to build houses for poor rural families. The little housing area would be called Koinonia Village. Throughout the area, tenant farmers were being forced off the land by mechanization and left with nowhere to go. We wanted to make a "village" for these people, providing them with decent dwellings in which to live.

We would solicit gifts and no-interest loans from benefactors and would charge no interest and make no profit from the new homeowners. The "Fund for Humanity" was created.

The first house was to be built for Bo and Emma Johnson. Largely uneducated and landless, descendants of slaves who once populated the surrounding farms, there was no way they—and others like them—could go into town and get a loan from a bank to build a house. Only a program taking into consideration the limited incomes of people like Bo and Emma could meet their need for housing offering terms they could afford to pay. And that's just what we did.

Their family lived across the road from Koinonia Farm in a shack with no plumbing or insulation. A few light bulbs hung from exposed wire. All around Koinonia were shacks like the Johnsons'—dirty, ramshackle dwellings where people lived with no hope of ever affording anything better. Our plan was to build houses for the poor around us; we were determined to get rid of those shacks.

(Photo by Ray Scioscia)

After a hard day's work too many families come home to shacks like this one.

Looking around the Johnsons' shack, I remembered the first time I'd ever worked on building a house and had a sense of dejá vu, realizing my first experience with a hammer might be one of the reasons I liked this idea of Partnership Housing so much. When I was ten, my father bought a four-hundred-acre farm, which was eight miles out in the country from our home in Lanett. The land was poor, with lots of swamps and rocky hillsides. Even the lumber had been cut by a work crew of German prisoners of war who had been interned in a nearby camp. On the farm were two shacks, much like the shacks still being lived in around Koinonia Farm. Both were dilapidated and unpainted.

An elderly couple, Bud and Mattie Lancaster, lived in the first house. My dad, I remembered, had listened compassionately as Bud pointed out the problems with the house and the water well that had caved in. My father scrutinized Bud's house, then eyed the other shack where the Glazes lived. He thought he could renovate Bud's house but the other shack was too far gone. The Glazes left the worst shack, and within a year it collapsed.

On Bud's house, though, we set to work. The house was a battered box consisting of two rooms and a hall. There was a front door for coming and going, and a back door for tossing out dishwater and spitting out snuff juice. It had no ceiling. The interior walls were just the backs of planks. The ancient roof was full of holes, so riddled that on rainy days Bud didn't have enough buckets to catch all the drips. I remember my dad saying it was going to be a major job to get the dwelling into decent shape, but I was eager to get going on it even at age ten.

We shored up the foundation with new columns of concrete blocks by banging some blocks under the house, then going inside and jumping up and down to see if the floor still shook. Next we ripped off the tattered roof and put on a new one. Then my Dad obtained some huge plywood boxes that had been packing cases for coffins and used the wood for ceilings and inside walls. After patching holes in the floor, we painted the whole house a shade of electric pink that Bud and Mattie loved. They were ecstatic. They had never lived in anything so beautiful as this colorful, coffin-carton shored-up shack, and I'll never forget that happiness. I could feel it coming at me and filling me up with happiness too, even at that young age.

What I learned from that first renovation has always stayed with me, and easily floated back into my mind as I studied Bo and Emma's shack. This time, though, instead of just making an old farm shack a little more livable, I was going to help a couple much like Bud and Mattie live in a brand-new house that was going to be theirs.

What was that first house like? A solid, concrete-block house built at a cost of six thousand dollars to be repaid each month for twenty years with no interest. A very simple house, it was nevertheless a palace compared to their old shack. It included a modern kitchen, a good heating system, and an indoor bathroom. Their monthly mortgage payment was twenty-five dollars, paid to the Fund for Humanity. Bo signed the mortgage with an "X."

For five years, we steadily built houses. And oh, how we could see the difference—a dramatic difference—that decent housing made in people's lives—and we could see it in the time it took for them to move in. Can you imagine what it's like the first night you've ever slept in a warm house? A house that has indoor plumbing? A house that is by some miracle really yours? How could you not be changed?

Before we'd finished the first house, Clarence Jordan died suddenly of a heart attack. But Linda and I continued the building project, pouring our passion into the building of those houses. In 1972 after Koinonia Village was completed, Linda and I decided to continue right on building. A new development was launched a few hundred yards from the first one. It would have even more houses. But, local leadership was adequate to keep the building going.

(Habitat for Humanity file photo)

Millard Fuller during a speech to dedicate a house built by Koinonia Partners.

We were offered a chance to test the housing concept in a radically different but incredibly needy place—a place we'd visited: Zaire. The Christian Church (Disciples of Christ), in association with the United Church of Christ, offered a special assignment for us to try partnership housing in that country. So we packed up the kids again, by now four of them with the birth of daughters Faith and Georgia, and headed overseas for three years.

Zaire's cities were teeming with miserable overcrowded settlements caused by the influx of villagers to the cities following independence from Belgium in 1960. Decent housing for anyone but the well-to-do was virtually impossible to find. They certainly needed what we were offering, if we could make it work.

What was it like? For three years Linda and I wrestled with problems and discouragements ranging from thievery, ludicrous bureaucracy, capricious arrests, and a perpetual shortage of funds and materials—as well as the cultural adjustment of being suddenly in a country where time means next to nothing. But we were blessed with a succession of great volunteers from the U.S. and Canada, and as soon as the local citizens saw we were serious, their enthusiasm knew no bounds.

From 1973–1976 we worked in Mbandaka, the capital city of Equator Region, building simple, decent cement-block houses for people who had been living in stick-and-mud shacks. No one in America or Europe would have lived in our houses. They were one-story structures—no electricity and no plumbing—with cement-slab floors and tin roofs, several bedrooms, and a separate kitchen area to keep the wood fire from smoking up the other rooms. But they had no vermin-infested thatch roofs nor mosquito-breeding puddles on dirt floors. And they had no mud walls to be slowly disintegrated by every storm that beat against them.

I'll never forget the words of a local pastor who lived in a crumbling mud house in one of the poorest neighborhoods in the city. As he was showing visitors our work site one day, he said, "Years ago, when missionaries came, the first thing they did was build nice houses for themselves. Next, they built nice houses for God. But," he said, waving his arms, "they didn't help the people build houses!" We built one for his family, though, and for many more families.

And the simple houses have lasted. When Linda and I went back to visit several years later, we found literally hundreds of well-kept houses, filled with grateful people.

We returned to Georgia in 1976, excited by how partnership house-and-community building had passed its overseas test with flying colors. The idea worked beyond Georgia's borders. Everyone needed simple, decent places to live—*everyone*.

Soon, we were hosting a group of twenty-six people at Koinonia from all over the United States and a dear colleague from Zaire, in a planning session to form a new organization to continue this crazy new idea we'd pioneered. One small delegation was from San Antonio, Texas. They had been inspired by the work at Koinonia and Zaire and were already making plans to build on their needy west side.

So, at Koinonia, building on the experience there and in Zaire, we forged the philosophy behind all we build and do today in Habitat for Humanity. No-interest, no-profit housing built by volunteers along with the new homeowners, bought with a monthly payment they could afford, without a penny from the government for the homebuilding—that was how we had done it and how we would continue to do it.

We packed up the kids and moved again . . . this time into town, to Americus . . . to begin.

Habitat for Humanity was launched. We had no idea how fast it would take off or where it would go.

That was almost twenty years ago. And the last two decades have been such a thrilling ride that sometimes Linda and I both have had to hold on tight. But we have.

Together.

CHAPTER THREE

How Did It Grow So Fast?

Habitat's First Twenty Years

YOU'RE GOING to walk *where?*"

Linda thought I had lost my senses. I wasn't sure she was wrong. But Habitat for Humanity was about to observe its seventh birthday. We needed something unusual and dramatic to gain some public exposure.

And I had an idea.

Habitat for Humanity had been growing steadily. At first the headquarters of Habitat for Humanity International was in my law office, the office—fittingly—being an old house we had renovated, the first of many we would renovate in that same dilapidated Americus neighborhood. Soon, we would be so big that I would walk away from my law practice once again.

We were amazed at how things were growing. The work had begun in Georgia and moved to Zaire, on the other side of the world. Then it had quickly spread to Texas, Guatemala, Florida, Uganda, South Carolina, and Tennessee (and eventually would be in all fifty states and dozens of other nations). Sometimes it seemed almost like Habitat was spreading on its own.

Today, I'm asked frequently whether I've been surprised about the phenomenal success of Habitat for Humanity. I always answer by saying, "Yes" . . . and "No." "No," because the idea was one that made too much sense—in every sense—not to work. But "Yes," because I'm surprised how it has taken root in so many different places—not only in the United States but also around the world. When we first began, we had a vision for Habitat to grow and expand, but our idea of expansion was limited to primarily a work in the rural South and a few developing countries. What has been so surprising is how it works in Bombay, India and Mexico City as well as in Lexington, Kentucky and Green Bay, Wisconsin and Eureka, California. It seems to work well anywhere, the only exception being in the inner cities of mega-cities, and we've even had some success stories there. (Also in 1995, we launched our Urban Initiative, with concerted efforts in Newark, Philadelphia, Cleveland, and Baltimore to bolster our work in the big cities.)

Back then, though, standing in the front doorway of our home in Americus, Georgia and contemplating seven years of unbelievable Habitat growth, all I knew was that it had been working faster and smoother in our first seven years than we had ever imagined. Now seemed an opportune moment for a big jump—the perfect time for some big media exposure. Habitat needed something sensational to spotlight its upcoming birthday.

On that day in early April 1983, I was thinking about a "big event" that would begin a legacy of fun, exciting, big-thinking Habitat events promoting our astronomical growth: A walk. A long walk.

How long?

A walk all the way from Americus to Indianapolis—a distance of seven hundred miles, where in September we'd planned to celebrate Habitat's birthday in conjunction with our fall board meeting. I thought walking that long distance would certainly attract media attention. To be honest, I had my doubts whether I could actually walk that far.

So on that Sunday in April, to test my strength, I stepped off my front steps in Americus to walk the eight miles to Koinonia Farm to attend Sunday afternoon worship. The service was at 4:00 P.M.; it was now nearly 2:00 P.M. The weather did not look good. Still, I told Linda, "I'm walking to the Koinonia service."

"You're going to walk *where?*" came her reply. "Why in the world are you walking *out there?*"

"I'll tell you later. I'll ride back with you." I grabbed a cap and an umbrella and left.

At about four miles, the rain started in earnest and so did the wind. At 3:45, drenched and totally exhausted, I turned into Koinonia's driveway. My legs were shaking and so was my resolve. But the next day I was not as sore as I thought I would be, so I was back to thinking again about actually walking seven hundred miles.

And when she saw I was serious, so was Linda.

We began to condition for the walk by, of course, walking. We were determined to do it.

(Habitat for Humanity file photo)

Millard and Linda Fuller prepared for months to be ready to lead the seven-hundred-mile walk to Indianapolis.

We charted out a five-mile course around Americus and faithfully walked it every evening. We were amazed at how quickly our bodies strengthened. We also discovered it took us almost exactly one hour to walk three miles. As we practiced walking, we did some calculations.

Walking six to seven hours, we could cover approximately twenty miles per day which, including a few rest days, would allow forty days to walk from Americus to Indianapolis.

Twenty miles a day, I thought. *We'd better increase the number of miles on our training program.*

So by mid-May, we were rising at five o'clock in the morning to walk five miles before breakfast. Our motto became "No pain, no gain." Then, we would walk five miles again in the evening either before or after dinner. On weekends, we did longer stints . . . nine miles, eleven miles . . . and right before time to begin the long walk, we walked fifteen miles a day for four consecutive days. We felt ready!

We had already announced our plans for the seven-hundred-mile walk, so we realized there was no backing out now. Gifts and pledges began to come in, as did volunteers to transport sleeping bags, do our cooking, and lend general logistical support. A few people emerged, too, who wanted to walk with us—some to the city limits, others to Atlanta, and even a few who wanted to go the full distance. Still others said they would join us along the way to walk various segments of the long trek. We even had volunteers who scouted the whole way, taking extensive notes about landmarks and towns along the route as well as making arrangements ahead with churches for places to sleep. Our overall fund-raising goal for the Seventh Anniversary Celebration was a million dollars, with the walk itself planned to generate a tenth of it—one hundred thousand dollars.

As we were making last-minute preparations for the walk to begin, we learned that Rosalynn Carter and her daughter Amy would join us to walk from our headquarters to the north edge of town. That caused a great deal of excitement. We tied up our shoelaces and started up the road with a group of walkers as crazy as Linda and me, ready to give their "soles" for the Habitat cause.

As we took our first steps through our own hometown, I remembered the last time I had led a walk up the main street of Americus. In August 1971, the black citizens of Americus had become incensed over instances of police brutality. Meetings were being held in black churches all over town, and a protest walk was planned around the court house. Several of us from Koinonia, after investigating the complaints, joined the cause.

Since then, times had changed remarkably. That day we walked, not as a crowd of blacks with a few whites, protesting what whites were doing to blacks, but as a totally integrated group. The mayor, the police chief, a former first lady, and a black city councilman walked with us to celebrate what we had been doing together to help one another.

What was it like to walk seven hundred miles? Blisters, thunderstorms, swarms of gnats, barking dogs, impromptu parades, the exhilaration and exhaustion of doing something challenging to mind and body, and the thrill of seeing America the way few people see it— at five miles per hour—that was the experience. And, oh yes, we got attention, if not as much media exposure as I had hoped. People along

(Habitat for Humanity file photo)

The walk to Indianapolis started with a procession through Habitat's hometown—Americus, Georgia. Rosalynn and Amy Carter helped get us underway.

the way heard about Habitat as we passed slowly through their towns. Only four of us finished the whole walk, but hundreds participated. And we made our goal of raising awareness as well as all the money we had projected. Immediately I began thinking about a walk to Kansas City, Missouri for Habitat's tenth anniversary in 1986. But I didn't tell Linda about that right away.

A year or so passed. I began to talk about walking again. The second walk, though, would have a higher aim—a thousand miles this time— and a goal of a million dollars, as part of an overall goal of ten million dollars. As you've probably gathered by now, I love seemingly impossible goals. I find they inspire people. "Make no little plans," as I love to quote. And I was right. This time, building on the first walk's success, imaginations—and the media—were captured.

The first walk, as I mentioned, received hardly any press. But the second one . . . that was going to be a very different story. We had acquired a presidential partner by that time and the media was, as they say, "alerted." We were set.

The summer of 1986 came. On the day we started, we could already tell this walk was going to be a smash-hit. Walkers came from across the country and from around the globe—including Costa Rica, Zaire, Papua New Guinea, Bolivia, India, Uganda, Peru, Germany, and Ireland. Jimmy and Rosalynn Carter walked the first nine miles to Plains with us. More than six hundred people poured out into the street from our Habitat headquarters parking lot, banners flying. We had three goals:

- walk a thousand miles and raise a million dollars for Habitat
- raise consciousness about shelter so more people would join our efforts
- get everybody to Kansas City alive and well with no injuries.

For seven weeks we walked and traversed the thousand miles to Kansas City, battling 110-degree heat. We ate meals along the highway under huge trees, slept in churches and campgrounds and civic centers, drank free soft drinks donated by grocery stores, and ate home-cooked meals prepared by local organizations and churches. We were served and ate so much ham that we started calling it "hamma," remembering the "manna" that the Israelites ate on their long walk to the Promised Land. We marched in parades, were escorted by horseback riders, held rallies with local dignitaries and congressmen, nursed sore sunburned bodies and blistered feet, were serenaded by gospel choirs, showered mercifully with fire engine hoses, held a wedding, welcomed people who joined us at the spur of the moment, and made the kind of friends you keep for a lifetime.

And at the end, in Kansas City, to begin our tenth anniversary celebration, the cameras were rolling as Jimmy and Rosalynn Carter greeted us along with the Governor of Kansas, the Secretary of State of Missouri, and other dignitaries. We raised a million dollars on this walk and surpassed our overall ten-million-dollar goal by over two million dollars! And, we got a billion dollars worth of free national publicity.

My good friend Tony Campolo—sociology professor at Eastern College in St. Davids, Pennsylvania, author, speaker par excellence, and

then member of Habitat for Humanity International's board of directors—delivered a moving talk to the assembled throng. Gesturing
dramatically in his characteristic manner, he exhorted, "We are not just
about building houses. . . . Habitat is building the kingdom of God. It is
taking people who think they're nothing and helping them discover that
they are something!"

Then Jimmy Carter, speaking in his usual low-key manner, delivered a
powerful message. At its conclusion, he announced that he and Rosalynn
were totally committed to the growing work of Habitat for Humanity.

The final speech of the celebration was given by David Rowe, president of the board of Habitat for Humanity International. He looked to
the future as he spoke:

> "The success of our next ten years will be directly traceable to our
> ability to find, win, and put to work those people who sigh and
> groan, and teach them to shout and sing! We need people who will
> start out to walk, but won't mind stopping to stoop down. We need
> people who will stoop down, but then won't mind cleaning up. And
> we need people, who after cleaning up, won't mind straightening up
> again and keeping moving. We need people who realize that spiritu-
> al ain't worth spit without sweat."

By any measuring standard, both the 1986 walk and the celebration
were roaring successes. But what next? We had tremendous momentum
and I wanted to keep it going. We had to, because with each new idea,
an incredible number of new houses were being built.

And that gave me the idea for an encore.

During a press conference in Kansas City, I announced our next big
event. We would build an *entire city block* in a week at the 1987 Jimmy
Carter Work Project in Charlotte, North Carolina.

Soon after that, we decided the event needed to be within a bigger
context, so we set a goal to build a thousand houses that same year. Even
though by 1987 we had added scores of new affiliates, we'd never built
more than five hundred houses in a year—and here I was, making us
stretch again. But it worked, as it always seemed to. Habitat volunteers'
hearts had proven over and over again to be as big as Habitat's dreams.

The idea that made it happen was the one that came next. Why
couldn't other Habitat affiliates also build *at the same time?*

So the week of the Jimmy Carter Work Project became "Habitat House-Raising Week," in which Habitat affiliates all over the world would be blitz-building at the same time.

Bob Hope gave a benefit in Charlotte that netted over thirty thousand dollars and with the golf club-shaped hammer given to him by Jimmy Carter, he bent his first nail as we cheered him on. At the end of the week, fourteen tired but incredibly happy families moved into completely finished houses. And the reports began to come in about the other House-Raising projects. More than two hundred Habitat affiliates had participated, building, renovating, or helping to repair more than three hundred houses in just five days. Some were finished that week and others would be completed in the weeks ahead. When the final tally was in at the end of the year, we'd exceeded our one-thousand-house goal by two hundred houses.

The media exposure and the grass-roots response were phenomenal. Things were happening—and happening fast.

(Photo by Carolyn Meritt)

Former President Jimmy Carter and legendary comedian Bob Hope share a funny moment during the 1987 Jimmy Carter Work Project in Charlotte, North Carolina.

Now we were ready for some new challenges. Why not put the two ideas together? Why not a Habitat *House-Raising Walk?* That's exactly what we did in 1988.

We combined the Jimmy Carter Work Project concept, the House-Raising idea, and a marathon consciousness-raising walk. The event would not only be a twelve-hundred-mile walk to celebrate twelve years of Habitat for Humanity, but it would also be a "traveling work camp." Starting in Portland, Maine, walkers and builders would cover twelve hundred miles over a period of twelve weeks, raising $1.2 million. Along the way, they would build or help renovate 120 houses. President Carter would split his time between two Work Projects—one in Philadelphia, where he would help renovate five apartments, and the other in Atlanta, building twenty new houses. The House-Raising Walk '88 would conclude in Atlanta, where the Twelfth Anniversary Celebration would be held.

(Photo by Ray Scioscia)

Jimmy Carter delivered a powerful message of support during Habitat's closing celebration for its House-Raising Walk in 1988.

The busy event drew near, and when the day arrived, everybody started walking and building. Down the east coast we came, pounding pavement and nails in an unforgettable twelve-week drama. Builders would get in vehicles on weekends and drive south approximately a hundred miles, then blitz-build for a week at a local Habitat affiliate. On Saturdays, the walkers would arrive at the building site to dedicate the Habitat houses built that week. Over the weekend, walkers and builders would participate in Habitat rallies, speak in churches, and spread the message of Habitat in every other way possible. This scenario was repeated each week—all the way to Atlanta.

The theme song for the walk was "Marching to Zion," the same song used on previous walks. It was special to Linda and me because it was the song we had sung over and over on the airplane when we flew home from New York following our reconciliation. On this walk, the song was doubly meaningful because in Clarence Jordan's "Cotton Patch" books, Jerusalem—known as Zion in Scripture—was Atlanta. So, we were literally marching to Zion! It was so meaningful and so exciting.

The song goes like this:

> *"Come, we that love the Lord*
> *And let our joys be known.*
> *We're marching to Zion,*
> *Beautiful, beautiful Zion.*
> *We're marching upward to Zion,*
> *That beautiful city of God."*

There were countless unforgettable things that happened along the way but two were especially memorable among the many wonderful experiences we had. In Philadelphia, although hundreds of people worked on the project, the response was less than enthusiastic. In separate interviews, Jimmy Carter and I expressed our disappointment in this lack of local support. The result was several news articles and one powerful cartoon that appeared in the *Philadelphia Daily News*.

There also was a moment in Philadelphia that moved me deeply— one of those frozen-in-time moments that seemed to stop everything and define all the effort and hopes and dreams we had been working for. One of the rallies that week was held at Bright Hope Baptist Church. A mezzo-soprano named Marietta Simpson sang "Bless This House" in the most incredible rendition of that song any of us had ever heard. I can still hear it, and it still moves me.

(Reprinted from the *Philadelphia Daily News*, Signe Wilkinson. Used by permission.)

From Philadelphia, I flew to Atlanta to participate in the Jimmy Carter Work Project there. Meanwhile, the walkers and builders continued their building journey southward. In Atlanta, twelve hundred builders had already gotten all the walls up by the time I arrived. Trusses were on, decking nailed down, and shingles in place on at least a third of the houses. Scores of churches had joined the city-wide effort to provide a huge chunk of the money and hundreds of volunteers. Peachtree Presbyterian Church had caught Habitat fever so thoroughly that the congregation made a five-year commitment to raise a hundred thousand dollars a year and provide a thousand volunteers to help rebuild an entire neighborhood in Atlanta. *That's* what we call "habititis."

A great example of how "the fever" can inspire and transform anyone it grabs is a man named John Wieland. An Atlanta businessman and homebuilder, John Wieland was owner of a company that built six of the twenty homes at the Jimmy Carter Work Project with his own people. During that time, he caught "habititis" so severely that he soon formed a not-for-profit division of his company, John Wieland Homes, to continue helping Habitat for Humanity in Atlanta while assisting other nonprofit groups dedicated to helping with the Atlanta housing crisis.

I flew back to the walk, and two of the highlights of that part of the experience were spending the night at a shelter for the homeless in Chester, Pennsylvania, then walking into Washington, D.C. and marching from the Capitol to the Lincoln Memorial. Andrew Young, then mayor of Atlanta, was with us and spoke to the walkers and builders from the Memorial's steps.

In the weeks following, the walkers slowly made their way south, joining with volunteers along the way to build houses in Richmond, Durham, Wake Forest, Greensboro, Asheville, Spartanburg, Carrollton, and a dozen more Southern cities on the way to Atlanta. When we finally walked into Atlanta, Jimmy Carter greeted us at the Carter Presidential Center, and then we finished our long walk at the Atlanta Civic Center where we later would host celebration activities. We'd finished our walk—twelve hundred miles, fourteen states, 154 new houses, and no serious injuries—that is, not counting the blisters on top of blisters. We were ready for our Twelfth Anniversary Celebration, tired but triumphant, and we had a ball.

When I spoke at the celebration, I quoted from the great Broadway musical, *Man of LaMancha*, in which Don Quixote and his little servant Sancho were arguing. Sancho insisted that facts were facts until Don Quixote screamed: "*Facts are the enemy of the truth!*" That has always spoken to me. We are always dealing with facts, but facts often can obscure the truth.

As I explained that night, the *fact* was that along the way on the House-Raising Walk, we'd been sore, tired, sometimes depressed by the length of the road, and even misunderstood on occasion. One man yelled from his car window as he passed, "Get a job!"

Those were the *facts*.

But what was the *truth?*

The *truth* was that we had a job to do—eliminate poverty housing and homelessness from the earth.

The *fact* is that Habitat could never build enough houses for everybody.

The *truth* is that we were becoming a conscience to the world, inspiring others to join us in this noble struggle. Everyone, working and building together, could accomplish the task.

The *fact* is that Habitat's approach of faith-inspired, no-profit, no-interest house-building using sweat equity and volunteers is naive and makes no sense. It can't possibly work.

The *truth* is that the idea came from God. God's ways are not our ways, but they are right. When we try them, we are amazed at how well the naive, nonsensical approach works.

The *fact* is that considering the immensity of the problem and the complexity of the situation, we cannot possibly hope to succeed in what we're trying to do.

But the *truth* is that, with God, all things are possible. "And, partners," I told the crowd, "we are marching ever onward in lock-step with the Lord God Almighty."

We've had fun coming up with numerous events to stir up homebuilding excitement to help the local affiliate cause, and they've all worked wonderfully. For instance, for our Fifteenth Anniversary in 1991, we had another blitz build—this time across America, starting in Tijuana, Mexico and fourteen other points around the perimeter of the United States. Each of those fifteen groups blitz-built their way over fifteen weeks, to arrive in Columbus, Ohio for the Fifteenth Anniversary Celebration. At least fifteen hundred houses were completed or worked on during that tremendously busy summer.

We had another grand parade into downtown Columbus to start the celebration. Over six thousand people were in attendance at the main Habitation on Friday night when Jimmy Carter spoke.

We've blitzed houses to celebrate the landmark goals of twenty thousand and thirty thousand houses built by Habitat for Humanity. In 1993, we

called the first one the 20/20,000 project. In a five-day blitz build of twenty houses in Americus, the twentieth house built was that milestone 20,000th house. Next was the 30/30,000 challenge, which had us building the 30,000th house as a part of a week-long, thirty-house blitz build— also in Americus, in 1994.

We've even built the fastest house ever built on record with Jack Kemp's help in five hours, fifty-seven minutes, and thirteen seconds. More than three hundred workers circled the Pensacola, Florida house site at 6:30 A.M. when we started with Linda leading a prayer; the house was finished by noon, complete with landscaping. We set a large navy-regulation

(Photo by Chris McGranahan)

Former HUD Secretary Jack Kemp lends a hand on Habitat's fastest-ever-built house in Pensacola, Florida.

electronic clock on the front lawn and watched it tick as we worked until the

(Habitat for Humanity file photo)

Millard Fuller announces Habitat's new construction record in Pensacola.

last moment when someone hit the "stop" button. We were tired, but delighted to see that we had set a new record, breaking the previous record of five hours, fifty-nine minutes set in Nashville in 1990. I jokingly told everyone we were going to keep building these houses faster and faster . . . until we finally got one finished before we even started!

Sometimes the event came to us. We knew we'd arrived as part of the American cultural scene when a mobile American history classroom stopped in Americus to help build a house. University of New Orleans professor Douglas Brinkley educates a lucky group of college students each year in a highly original way. He takes a college class around the country in his "Majic Bus" to experience America first-hand, exploring America's literary and historical landscape. Sometimes they get to be a part of this landscape as they study it, which was the case when Dr. Brinkley chose a Habitat for Humanity building project as one of their stops. The group—college students from the University of New Orleans, Tulane University, University of Virginia, Kenyon College, American University, Haskell Indian Nations College, Yale, and New York University—spent four days blitz building with us. When they left, a house was standing. As Stacy James, a junior at Haskell Indian College in Kansas, expressed, "That is the greatest kind of impact to make."

The Majic Bus rolled into Americus in 1994, filled with college students on an amazing journey of learning by doing.

Denver Broncos quarterback John Elway (left) takes a break during the "Home Improvement" taping in Atlanta.

Another important event was the Super Bowl Blitz Build in January 1994. National Football League players and other celebrities teamed up with the Atlanta Habitat for Humanity to build four houses in the days leading up to Super Bowl XXVIII. Billy Joe Tolliver of the San Diego Chargers, Mike Haynes of the Atlanta Falcons, Glyn Milburn and John Elway of the Denver Broncos, Eric Turner of the Cleveland Browns, and Warren Moon of the Houston Oilers were the football volunteers. Also wielding a hammer was 1994 Miss America Kimberly Aiken. Participating in media events were World

(Photo by Chris McGranahan)

Houston Oilers quarterback Warren Moon was a key player in the Super Bowl Blitz Build in Atlanta in 1994.

Heavyweight Boxing Champ Evander Holyfield, Dr. Loretta Long from PBS-Television's "Sesame Street," and former HUD secretary and former pro football player Jack Kemp. Clips of the project were shown inside the stadium during the Super Bowl. And during it all, the ABC television series "Home Improvement" was filming on the site. Afterward, the cast and crew gave Habitat a check for ten thousand dollars.

When all the Super Bowl excitement was over, the excitement inside the new Habitat homes was just beginning. Ronald Cullins, his wife Anna, and their seven children are just one of the families that moved into the

(Photo by Mark McQueen)

1994 Miss America Kimberly Aiken with a new Habitat family.

real reason for all the work. They moved from Culver Homes, a government project—where they feared for their children's lives every day, where two of their children saw a teenager shot dead, where they came home shaking with fright because they could hear gunfire all the time. But Ronald worked alongside these famous football players to build his family a new life, and he put in his own sweat equity on Ida Blackwell's house, his new neighbor-to-be. In the *Chicago Tribune,* where Ronald was interviewed by sports columnist Bob Verdi, the new homeowner said, "Man, I've been through it all. Drugs, divorce, you name it. I'm a black man who can't buy a ticket to see the Falcons. What's a Super Bowl ticket, $175? No way. But I've got trees now and grass, and I've got a chance. . . . After the game is over and all the fancy people leave town, I can say thanks for my trees."

For 1995's Super Bowl XXIX in Miami, we did it again. This time National Football League Players Neil Smith, Calvin Williams, Glyn Milburn, and former Green Bay Packer Ray Nitschke pitched in to help Habitat for Humanity at two different locations. Smith and Nitschke created some fun and excitement by helping volunteers with Habitat for Humanity of Greater Miami construct the front section of a steel frame house at the NFL Experience at Joe Robbie Stadium. This section was later partially disassembled and moved to a house already under construction in South Miami Heights.

Just a few miles away in Hallandale, Williams and Milburn joined hundreds of other volunteers with Habitat for Humanity of Broward County to complete four homes in partnership with local families in need before the kick-off on Super Bowl Sunday.

Then there was "The Road to L.A." To celebrate our eighteenth anniversary at Loyola Marymount University in the Los Angeles area, August 4–6, 1994, we planned a ten-month series of special events throughout the nation and the world, calling it "The Road to L. A." The event was kicked off in October 1993, with the Charlotte, North Carolina affiliate blitz build. The house count: twenty-two. (In 1994, Habitat for Humanity of Charlotte was the first affiliate in the United States to reach the two-hundred-house milestone.) The January Super Bowl XXVIII Blitz Build in Atlanta started things off right in 1994: four houses. In June, the 30/30,000 Blitz Build in Americus put up our 30,000th house by completing thirty houses in one week. In the first two weeks of July, Delta Sigma Theta, the country's largest African-American service sorority, blitzed fifteen houses into existence in St. Louis, Missouri and East

St. Louis, Illinois. That exciting event was part of their annual meeting, where they made further plans for their significant partnership with Habitat for Humanity, encouraging sponsorship and building wherever they have chapters and even expanding their interest to Africa and the Bahamas. A week later, the annual Jimmy Carter Work Project, led by former president and Mrs. Carter took place at the Cheyenne River Sioux Indian Reservation in Eagle Butte, South Dakota, the first time a Jimmy Carter Work Project was held on a Native American reservation. House count: thirty. And then finally Los Angeles, where Celebration '94 took place in August at the end of "The Road to L.A." Volunteers blitz-built a house, conducted seminars, and deepened Habitat's commitment to education and training at every level of our organization.

For our historic Twentieth Anniversary Celebration in 1996, we will take a nostalgic walk from Americus to Atlanta, site of the Twentieth Anniversary Celebration. While I'm with hundreds of walkers from Americus to Atlanta, a throng of bicyclists will ride from Canada to Kentucky and link up with more bicyclists for the ride to Atlanta. Jerry and Cindy Schulz, super Habitat partners from Olympia, Washington, plan to walk from Olympia to Atlanta. That's a three-thousand-mile, seven-month commitment! They will leave February 1 to arrive for the Labor Day Weekend Celebration in Atlanta. We are expecting several thousand people—and lots of excitement. The 50,000th Habitat house will be built by that anniversary date, and maybe even the 60,000th house too.

These thousands of houses, built over a span of almost twenty years . . . how did they fare in some of the worst weather the world has seen in the last century?

In other words, how good really is a house built by volunteers?

Hurricane Andrew, which decimated thousands of houses, didn't take down a single Habitat house. *That's* how good.

All twenty-seven houses built by Habitat for Humanity in south Florida were still standing with only the slightest of damage. And some were right

The 1994 Jimmy Carter Work Project was held on an Indian reservation—another "first."

in the hurricane's path. On Guava Street in west Perrine, all that was left of the neighborhood were splintered trees, trashed cars, headless palms, and yards full of debris which had once been houses. . . . except for four Habitat houses standing side by side in a sea of devastation. The *Miami Herald* headline about the sturdy Habitat houses proclaimed:

Tally: Habitat 27, Andrew 0.

"This is a six-day house, one built in six days—not six months," homeowner Al Taylor told a reporter.

Homeowner Larsen Griffin recalls personally nailing down the metal hurricane ties that anchor the roof. He remembers that there were doubters when Habitat offered to build sturdy frame homes in Perrine. Even the officials said they'd just as soon not have any Habitat homes unless they were built of concrete blocks because of the hurricanes. But as Griffin pointed out about those four Perrine houses, "All they did was rock with the wind."

I flew there to see for myself. The Habitat houses looked like they had been built *after* the hurricane. One house had a tree limb driven right through its roof, but that was the extent of the damage. Irma Cordero's house in Homestead was right in the eye of the storm. Everything

(Photo by Don Hall)

This Habitat house in Homestead, Florida suffered minor damage from devastating Hurricane Andrew in 1992. All twenty-seven Habitat houses in the Miami area survived the storm intact.

around her was utterly devastated. Yet here her house stood firm, with only a few windows broken and a small porch blown to parts unknown. Irma's son Carlos told me they evacuated the area along with everyone else, moving to a friend's house located a few miles north.

"It was scary," he said, shaking his head. He thought they were all going to die. As they drove back the next morning, he said his mother began to cry, "What are we going to do? Our house is gone!" When they turned the last corner, they could see the house was standing. His mother just kept right on crying. "The tears changed from sad ones to tears of happiness and thanksgiving," he explained with a smile.

Then in January 1994, a major earthquake hit Los Angeles. Eight Habitat houses were near the epicenter in the San Fernando Valley. The houses, all but finished and still unoccupied, were not damaged in any way, and other Habitat houses in the area were undamaged too.

How did they withstand such a force? That is a question reporters often ask me. There is a spiritual dimension, but it's not mysterious beyond comprehension. I think our houses are sturdy because our houses are built by volunteers who aren't so sure of themselves as builders. So when they are told to put two nails in a board, they put ten. And beyond the fact that we emphasize quality construction, volunteers' only pay is hearing, "*job well done*," and enjoying a sense of doing God's work so, of course, they are going to do it right.

That means we not only take the time to nail boards properly but install hurricane clips to roof trusses and place shingles correctly and tight. The same care in construction goes into blitz-built houses, even the fastest-built ones. Some of the Miami houses that withstood the hurricane gales were blitz-built in the 1990 Jimmy Carter Work Project. Those had been built of Styrofoam and wire grid "sandwich" sprayed with liquid concrete. The porch and houses were bolted to the foundation rather than nailed, a key to their sturdiness.

Right after the hurricane, we realized that by far the greatest number of victims were low-income people, many without insurance who had no means but their own hands to help rebuild their ravaged homes. So we pledged one million dollars in relief and began efforts to raise three to five million dollars for a "Hurricane Andrew Fund" for homebuilding. Even before we made the announcement, donations and offers to help reached our office for the stricken area. The U.S. Catholic Conference was ready to bus in fifty workers, and Habitat affiliates from North Dakota, Pennsylvania, and many other states quickly offered to help.

The California earthquake also urgently increased the need for Habitat building. So we began making plans to build more houses and assist the people whose homes were damaged by the earthquake, setting up an Earthquake Fund.

Then in the summer of 1994, just as our own 30/30,000 project in Americus had been finished and all thirty homeowners moved in, we received twenty-one inches of rain in twenty-four hours. The result was the worst flood in local recorded history.

Many people lost their homes and some even lost their lives. Friends of ours drowned or were injured. A couple we knew were literally blown through the back wall of their house by the force of the water. The husband survived by grabbing a tree as he was swept a quarter of a mile south of the house, but his wife was pulled under and drowned.

I knew the site of the new Habitat houses was on low-lying ground. As I drove toward the site at daybreak, my heart sank. A few blocks away was an absolute lake created by rainwater and runoff from a swollen creek. All the businesses, houses, and even the power station on the street were under water. Two houses were on fire on a little island in the lake and nothing could be done. Because the fire trucks couldn't get to them, they burned to the ground. I tried another route to the site, but the bridge was out, and I could see that a house was in the process of falling into the raging flood beside it.

Finally, I was able to get through by another route, and even though the tiny creek beside the Habitat houses was now a roaring river, not one house had been damaged. Of the 164 houses Habitat had built in Americus and Sumter County by that time, only four were flooded and none were structurally damaged.

One of the four homes flooded was a "Christmas house" that had been built during the holiday season two years earlier. When we built that particular one, we knew the land was below the one-hundred-year flood level, so we built the house up four feet above the specified flood level. When the 1994 flood hit, the water not only went up to the one hundred-year flood level but four feet above it—eight feet above the century mark.

Of course, once again, we moved into action to help those who had lost their homes and belongings in the flood. We virtually suspended our normal operations to help with relief efforts. The four Habitat houses that had been flooded were quickly repaired and the owners moved back in.

And as new Habitat houses were built in south Florida, Los Angeles, and Americus—as well as on the Hawaiian island of Kauai and along the Mississippi and Missouri Rivers—for victims of earthquakes, hurricanes, and floods, we continued to realize what an integral role our philosophy had played in restoring lives.

As the work in the United States has mushroomed, so has building all over the world.

In 1994 and 1995, Linda and I visited Habitat work in Central and South America, the Caribbean, and Africa. What we experienced on those long journeys was truly incredible and most heartwarming. Let me share some of that exciting work with you. I believe you'll be inspired, as we were, by what is happening in these farflung places in the rapidly expanding movement of Habitat for Humanity.

Our first trip in 1994 was to Bolivia and Brazil. In March, we visited our work in El Alto, Bolivia. Several dozen modest but good, solid houses had been completed there and many more were under construction. We also visited Santa Cruz, the country's largest city where nearly two hundred Habitat houses had been built. The homeowner families had held a lottery to see who would host us as their overnight guests. A single mom with two children and her mother won the lottery, so we spent the night in their little house. They gave up their bed for us. It rained during the night, but the house remained bone-dry. It filled our hearts with joy to realize what a good roof means to our Habitat families. In Brazil, we visited Belo Horizonte, where two hundred Habitat houses were nearing completion. Scores of Habitat families were working on their new houses. It was a thrill to see such effective mutual self-help in operation. From Belo we traveled to Piracicaba, a city some 130 kilometers northwest of Sao Paulo, where the government had just granted a large tract of land to the new Habitat affiliate for building up to one thousand houses. We held a grand ceremony to dedicate this new site.

Our next trip was in October to visit our work in the Dominican Republic, El Salvador, and Honduras. That trip started with a bang. Literally.

Linda and I were in northern New Jersey to participate in a sub-regional meeting of Habitat affiliates in the area and to speak at the Tenth Anniversary Celebration of Paterson, New Jersey Habitat for Humanity which was also, incidentally, a celebration to mark the completion of their fiftieth house. Following the afternoon meeting, we went to the home of one of our Habitat leaders to change clothes. Then, we were driven into the city of Paterson to tour the area where the Habitat houses had been built.

As we were leaving the Habitat neighborhood on our way to the church where I was to speak that night, our driver turned left at a red light and was broadsided by an oncoming car. I was in the right rear seat. The car that hit us smashed into our vehicle about a foot behind where I was sitting. The force of the impact threw me into the right rear door, which crammed my right arm into my rib cage. The wind was knocked out of me and some ribs were broken.

No one else was hurt. I did a self-assessment of my injuries and concluded that they were not life-threatening. I knew that broken ribs would eventually heal. I declined to go to the hospital in the emergency vehicle which came, sirens blaring, to the scene. Instead, someone pulled the bent side of the car away from the tire.

We drove directly to the dinner, where three hundred people were waiting for the events of the evening, and the speech was made, as planned.

The next morning, Linda and I left for the Dominican Republic. I was incredibly sore and couldn't carry anything, so Linda lugged our baggage and my heavy briefcase. At one point she exclaimed, "Millard, could you please drag a leg or do something to let people know there is something physically wrong with you?" In Miami, we met up with Dick Perry,

Latin America Area Director for Habitat for Humanity International. Linda was relieved to get his help with all those bags.

From outward appearances, I was just fine, but those ribs were incredibly sore and sensitive. The pain persisted throughout the trip, especially when we traveled on rough roads (which was often!) or when I coughed or sneezed. I could hear the ribs crunching when I breathed deeply. But over time, the pain diminished and I never missed a single engagement because of the injuries.

When we arrived in Santo Domingo, it was pouring rain. As we were driving into the city, our vehicle—a van—flooded out twice. Our Habitat hosts had to get out in the water, sometimes up to their knees, to push the van to dry ground. Finally, with great difficulty, we made it all the way to our destination in the city.

The next day, we drove west to the town of Barahona, the most active site of Habitat work in the Dominican Republic. It was a three-hour ride on a road that was paved but riddled with potholes!

In Barahona, twenty-five houses had been completed and thirty-two more were under construction. The nearby towns of Los Cocos and Enriquillo had already completed more than one hundred Habitat houses.

We stayed overnight with a Habitat family. The elderly grandmother was so very happy to have us as guests. She kept patting us on our arms and shoulders, all the time smiling broadly. Then she exclaimed, "I'm an ugly old woman, but I have a good heart!" And, indeed, she did have a good heart. It was a blessing to be the recipients of such love and attention. The next morning as we were getting ready to leave, she said, "When you visit again, I won't be here. I'll be in heaven."

From the Dominican Republic, we flew to El Salvador. In that war-torn country, Habitat had built more than two hundred houses. Many more were planned or under construction. We met in the capital city of San Salvador with the national committee of Habitat for Humanity. This dedicated group of men and women had been on both sides of the conflict that ravaged their country for more than a decade. Now, they were working together to build hundreds—and eventually thousands—of Habitat houses.

We drove northwest out of San Salvador to the town of Santa Ana, the town where most of our Habitat houses had been built. We stayed overnight in the little village of San Luis with a Habitat family by the name of Vasquez. We were served a wonderful meal of pupusas (tortillas with a choice of cheese or bean filling topped with shredded cabbage and a tangy sauce). We learned later that the family had rented a dining room table and chairs just for our visit, since they had so little furniture.

The family did not yet have their outdoor toilet dug, so we used a neighbor's toilet two doors down. We also used their bathhouse which was adjacent to the toilet. It was simply constructed of some long sticks which precariously held up pieces of cloth no more than four feet high. So I had to squat down partially or totally, then pour water over my head. At one point, when I had my head lathered with shampoo, Linda asked me to stand up so she could snap a picture. We had an audience by that time, so we added considerably to the amusement of the local people.

After breakfast we wandered up and down unpaved streets touring a dozen Habitat houses. As we popped in for brief visits, most of the women were in their neat, clean outdoor kitchens cooking tortillas. Two- and three-room houses were being built there at a cost of $1,100 to $1,500. The floors were covered with attractive tiles and the walls were made of red bricks. The roofs consisted of light gray tiles placed over construction iron rods that were attached to some long boards.

The tour ended at the local school where a big celebration had been planned, including the dedication of twenty-seven Habitat houses and afterward a big meal. Many people had come from surrounding areas where Habitat had already begun building houses or where building would soon begin.

The celebration was a wonderful occasion and included speeches by Linda and me, and others. In my talk, I said that Habitat for Humanity had come to El Salvador to be a healing force and to build houses as an expression of God's love. Linda gave out twenty-seven Bibles to the new Habitat homeowners. A highlight of the celebration was a group of men who sang for us while we ate.

The largest visiting group at the celebration was from a northern suburban area of San Salvador called Finca Argentina. Twenty-four houses had been completed there, including seventeen for families in which one or more members were blind. Twenty-one more houses, we learned, were under construction.

We visited Finca Argentina the next day. The blind families hosted us for a noon meal, after which a member from each family rose, one after the other, to express gratitude for their new Habitat houses. They explained that they earned their living making mattresses but that their meager incomes were not sufficient to build a house without help from a program like Habitat for Humanity. Many spoke with great emotion, amidst tears, but all were brief. Each person typically concluded their remarks by saying, "Solamente." That's Spanish for "only" or "that's all."

I reflected on those speeches in coming days and especially on how they ended their remarks. *Solamente.* Only that . . . Not much . . . But enough to meet one of their most basic needs. It reminded me of the simple words of Jesus about feeding the hungry, giving water to the thirsty, inviting strangers in, visiting the sick and the prisoners. Doing those simple things is not much—solamente—but those small things make such a big difference.

Last stop was Honduras. We first visited San Pedro Sula where Habitat was beginning to build in a neighborhood called Seis de Mayo, so named because a group of families invaded the land about ten years earlier on May 6. Today, the land is covered with hundreds of families who live in modest homes or little shacks up and down dirt streets. Habitat had completed eight houses there, and four more were under construction.

At a public meeting in the community, the president of the local Habitat Committee, a very thin young woman, tried to speak but became so emotional that she just had to leave the stage. Melvin Flores, our national coordinator in Honduras, told us that the woman had a very difficult life. He told of finding her in her shack a few weeks earlier, crying because she had not eaten for three days. He said he gave her some money so that she and her children could eat. In spite of her personal problems, she was giving leadership to the emerging Habitat work in her neighborhood.

We later visited her shack and saw blocks stacked there for her new Habitat house. Habitat houses in that community are an average of 350 square feet and cost one thousand dollars each. (We learned later that this young woman found a secretarial job, her Habitat house had been finished, and she and her children were happily ensconced in it.)

We continued on to the Yure River Basin, located south of San Pedro Sula. We drove to a small community called St. Elena. The Habitat houses there, like the ones in Seis de Mayo, were made of concrete blocks but, unlike the San Pedro Sula houses, they had no interior walls. The families, after they moved in, would finish the interiors as they chose and as they were able to do so.

We spent the night in St. Elena with a Habitat family. They had completed their interior walls, but did not yet have doors. At 4:30 A.M. we were awakened by loud music next door. We learned later that people in that area get up at that hour on a regular basis!

At noon that day we had a big Habitat rally in a nearby village. Several hundred people came from throughout the river basin area. Nearly three hundred Habitat houses had been finished by the time we visited.

Linda and I returned home, quite optimistic about the future of our work in the Dominican Republic, El Salvador, and Honduras. We saw the need was enormous in all three countries, but we knew we had talented, dedicated people working in the many locations where Habitat houses were being built, and plans already were in place to expand the work to many new locations. I was confident that we would build literally thousands of houses in those countries by the turn of the century.

In January 1995, we took off on another journey—this time to Africa to visit our work in the Central African Republic, Malawi, Ethiopia, and Egypt. In July, we were back on the continent to visit Zaire (for the twentieth anniversary of our work in that country), Botswana, and South Africa.

Habitat for Humanity is currently working in twelve countries in Africa, with plans to expand into several more over the next few years. On our two trips in 1995, we were able to see first-hand the exciting work in seven of the countries.

In the Central Africa Republic (C.A.R.), we bounced over rough and dusty roads to see our work in remote villages with exotic names like Bekadili, Dobèré, Baoro, and Koursou. As usual, we stayed with local Habitat families. In Bekadili, the bed collapsed. I had gotten in first as Linda was preparing for bed. I told her I thought the bed was unstable and might collapse. Just at that moment, it did! So, we just took it apart and put the thin mattress on the floor and slept like that during the night. About a dozen men sat right outside our window and talked around a fire all night long. They told us in the morning that they stayed there and talked so we wouldn't feel lonely!

We toured the village and saw the many Habitat houses that had been built. We also helped lay some blocks on a house that was under construction for a man named Vendredi John-Paul (Friday John-Paul). I was laughing and joking with him about his new house. I asked him what he thought about it. He replied that he thought about his new house all the time. I then commented to the crowd that he had a house in his head. Everyone laughed uproariously.

In Dobèrè, we had a huge outdoor church service, attended by all the Catholic and Protestant church members. In Baoro, Linda met separately with the women of the town. Our dedicated International Partner in C.A.R., Libbie Freed, lives in Baoro. From there, she helps guide the work in a total of nine villages in rural Central African Republic.

In Koursou, we held a big rally in the Baptist church. Nitu Kumba, our national director in C.A.R., told us that Habitat had done the most work in that village.

Under the good guidance of Nitu and Libbie, we completed more than two hundred houses in C.A.R. by the end of 1995. The work will continue to grow in the years ahead. One particular plan being promoted strongly by our capable Africa Area Director Harry Goodall (with whom we traveled on both trips), is to start a major work in the capital city of Bangui, in addition to expanding in the interior.

Next we visited Malawi. This small, long and thin nation located in southeastern Africa has built more Habitat houses than any other country in Africa. At the end of 1994, they had completed over two thousand houses in twelve locations, with twelve hundred more planned for 1995. Habitat for Humanity is the largest homebuilder in the country.

During our short trip, we visited Habitat work in Blantyre, the largest city, where in a suburban area called South Lunzu, we had built two hundred houses and had acquired land for three hundred more. We laid blocks there with Malawi's Minister of Housing, the Honorable T. S. Mangwazu, and had a ceremony to present Bibles to one hundred new Habitat homeowners.

We also visited Zomba, a very lovely town to the north of Blantyre. The plan was to dedicate the 200th Habitat house in a suburban area there, but it was raining and the roads were impassable. We went instead to a Habitat building site in the city where sixty-seven houses had been completed. They were located on a street that had been named Habitat Highway. The houses, made of red bricks with tile roofs, were very beautiful. Indeed, the whole area was quite picturesque, with a profusion of flowers, plots of lush green corn, and stately mountains in the background.

Linda and I stayed with a Habitat family in a rural area outside Zomba. In the evening, we went with them to their Baptist church and, by candlelight, had a lively service that continued until nearly midnight.

From Zomba, we drove northward toward the capital city of Lilongwe. Along the way, we stopped at Balaka, where eighty Habitat houses had been finished; they had land for eighty more.

In Lilongwe, we had the biggest event of our stay in the country. More than two thousand people, including the Minister of Housing and the U.S. Ambassador, attended a grand ceremony to dedicate the first house on a large plot of land given to Habitat for Humanity by the government. It was enough land to build four thousand houses. Nearly seven hundred Habitat houses had already been built elsewhere in the city, but on that particular piece of land—which, incidentally, was just ideal for houses— a virtual new city of thirty thousand people would rise over the next four or five years. It was exciting to be there!

In Ethiopia, we have work in the capital city of Addis Ababa and in Sodo, a town four hundred kilometers south of Addis Ababa. The work there is unique. Thirty-two houses were nearing completion for disabled families who worked for a local craft center. Like the blind families in El Salvador, the people were hard workers, but they did not make enough money to afford decent houses without a program like Habitat for Humanity. Linda and I had the joyous privilege of dedicating the first two houses that were nearing completion and presenting Bibles to the grateful families.

In Sodo, our energetic International Partner Kyle Jennings had been diligently working with local leaders to build the first forty-two houses. The first one was almost finished, so it was dedicated during our brief visit.

On the evening of our arrival, the local Habitat committee served us a wonderful feast. We found the food of Ethiopia to be absolutely delicious. Following the meal, we were presented clothing of nobility from the area. They insisted that Linda and I go to separate rooms and with persons assisting us, put on our new clothing. She returned first, wearing a bulky hand-loomed wool blanket around the lower part of her body and a thin blouse and scarves covering her torso. They told her the blanket could be used on her bed in winter. Very practical. My two-piece outfit was bright red. The v-neck top was sleeveless and the pant legs were calf length. When I walked in, Linda convulsed with laughter. She tried to contain herself, but it was impossible. Her laughter caused everyone in the entire room to laugh with her. It was some wild scene!

Another interesting episode in Sodo was meeting Baby Habitat. The chairman of the local Habitat committee was a fine man named Wubetu Tadeesa. While in Addis Ababa a few weeks earlier, his wife gave birth to a little boy. The father thought it only appropriate to name him "Habitat!" We met the little fellow and found him to be one bright-eyed little boy. It will be fun to keep up with his growth as Habitat for Humanity grows in his town and country.

Millard and Linda Fuller with Baby Habitat.

(Photo by Harry Goodall)

(Photo by Linda Fuller)

Millard Fuller with Coptic Orthodox Church Bishop Tadros—Habitat partner in Port Said, Egypt.

The last stop on our January trip was Egypt. We first visited Port Said on the Suez Canal, where we had begun work in partnership with the Coptic Orthodox Church to build two seven-story buildings, each for forty-two families. The first building was nearing completion, and we laid some of the first blocks for the second building.

In Cairo, we were working with the Coptic Evangelical Church. A total of thirty-three houses had been completed in one of the big garbage dumps in Cairo called Motamadia. Another one hundred were planned for completion in 1995. We spent most of one Sunday morning in this garbage dump visiting some of the seven thousand people who live there. As you can imagine, it was a sobering experience. The houses we built there were very modest and cost only nine hundred dollars each, but they enabled the people to have a little respite from the filth they lived in and sorted through for their survival, seven days a week.

From the garbage dump, we drove directly to one of the largest churches in Cairo—Kasr El Dobara Evangelical Church, where I had the privilege of preaching the morning sermon.

We returned to the United States the next day—exhausted, but full of hope for our extensive work in Africa, which would continue long after our tour of the various sites was just a memory. The July trip would be

exciting too, but that was nearly six months away.

A family awaiting a new Habitat house in the garbage dumps in Cairo.

(Photo by Linda Fuller)

Meanwhile, what was going on
back at the office? The work in
Africa and all around the
world, in addition to the ever-
expanding work in the United
States, was causing some
"growing pains." After almost twenty years, we were especially feeling
those growing pains at our headquarters on Church Street in Americus.
Even though by now we were taking up an entire city block, we were literally bursting at our seams.

Our headquarters in Americus, Georgia—a town of about seventeen thousand people in a small county in southern Georgia—is about
a two-and-half-hour drive from Atlanta. We've had quite a bit of pressure to relocate to a bigger city. But in Americus we can operate at a
fraction of the cost we would incur in a big city, and every cent we save
can go into building another house. Besides, we have done so much
work in Americus to eliminate poverty housing and like the idea of
seeing it through. So we decided to stay put and raised the money to
refurbish three inter-connected downtown buildings. Our old offices,
that we knew even years ago we would one day outgrow, would be converted into apartments for volunteers, just as we had envisioned.

All of the money was raised for the purchase and renovation of these
old downtown buildings through generous and timely donations, and our
new headquarters was dedicated on February 18, 1995. We now have the
elbow room we need to keep right on growing and building.

All this in twenty years.

How has it been accomplished?

In India, while giving a speech, I talked about how Habitat was a partnership with God, the homeowners, the local Habitat organization, and

the people in India, the United States, and other countries. "Anyone can be a partner," I said. "All you need is a loving heart and a desire to share and be a part."

Afterward, as we were walking through the crowd to our vehicle, a little girl appeared in front of me with her hand held out. I thought she was one of the many begging children in India, until I looked in her hand. She held some coins. I was startled for a second, then realized she was giving the money to me! I lifted this new little partner into my arms and announced to the crowd what she was doing. Then turning to our host, Father Aloysius, I said, "This little girl has given these rupees to me. I now want to give them to you to use in buying materials to build more houses for needy families." A cheer went up, the band began to play, and we jumped and danced and laughed as those few yet so very meaningful rupees went into the fund to pay for a new house in that little girl's community.

By the time you read this, we will have built our 40,000th house. This monumental milestone was reached in September 1995 as a part of a program called "Building on Faith."[1] The 40,000th house was blitz-built by Twin Cities Habitat for Humanity in St. Paul, Minnesota. Amazing, isn't it? We built ten thousand houses in less than a year. Right now, in more than twelve hundred American towns and cities and in over seven hundred locations in other countries, Habitat for Humanity volunteers are planning and building. And the plan calls for thirty-five to forty houses a day in 1995—that's twelve thousand to fifteen thousand houses. We will build twice that many in a single year by 1998. The sky's the limit. If my figures are right, we could house more than a million people within less than ten years: that is, if we continue to grow and work together at this phenomenal rate.

In 1985, only ten years ago, we built four hundred houses worldwide. In 1995, the most conservative estimate is that we will build twelve thousand houses. That's thirty times as many houses as we built in a year a

(Photo by Linda Fuller)

Millard Fuller and a new Habitat partner in Bangalore, India. This child's unselfish gift to Habitat India was a testament to the power of love in action. Notice the coins in Millard's hand.

decade ago. At that rate of growth, we will be building 360,000 houses a year by 2005! Even if the rate of growth slows to only a third of the rate of the past ten years, we'll build 120,000 houses a year ten years from now. Isn't that exciting?

So, houses for a million people? That sounds too conservative. How about five million? Why not even more?

CHAPTER FOUR

Who's That Swinging a Hammer?

Well-Known Habitat Volunteer Partners

IN BETWEEN THOSE first two long Habitat walks, we acquired our best-known volunteer, a partner who has done more than anyone else to gain us worldwide exposure and help make Habitat for Humanity a household name in the United States. The volunteer partner, of course, is Jimmy Carter. His wife Rosalynn has been right beside him in all of his work with Habitat for Humanity, as an equally committed and enthusiastic partner.

Every person involved in Habitat in any way is important to the work. Every letter written, every slide show presented, and every contribution—physical labor, a shared idea, a can of paint, or a gift of money—is immensely important. And every house built, renovated, or repaired in any one of the scores of Habitat affiliates around the world is a significant part of the process of sensitizing, inspiring and motivating people to get rid of the shacks and replace them with simple, decent places to live. Everyone is needed; each person, in his or her own unique way, contributes to the work and those contributions add up to make a difference.

But when a former president and first lady of the United States joined forces with us, the resulting impact was sudden and dramatic.

Our credibility was instantly established among the potential doubters across the country, and doors began to open much quicker and easier than ever before.

President Carter is our neighbor, living only nine miles from us—the distance between Americus and Plains. He first learned about Habitat for Humanity from neighbors in Plains who volunteered for two years with our Habitat program in Zaire in 1980. The Carters invited the family to spend a couple of days with them in the White House before they left for Africa. In 1982, President Carter accepted an invitation to speak to our board of directors, which was meeting in Americus. Later in the year, President and Mrs. Carter gave a generous donation to Habitat. But in 1983 when Rosalynn and Amy Carter helped launch our very first Habitat Walk, I decided that the Carters must be interested in what we were trying to accomplish in more than a peripheral way.

So, in keeping with my philosophy of "asking" rather than "not asking"—having learned that more happens when you ask than when you don't—I requested a meeting with the Carters. They cordially obliged. Sitting across from the former president and first lady in their home in Plains that day, I asked directly, "Are you simply *interested* in Habitat for Humanity, or are you *very interested?*"

President Carter smiled broadly, looked at Rosalynn and then quietly replied: "We're *very interested.*"

"Well," I responded, "what do we do with that interest?"

"Write me a letter," he suggested, "outlining ideas you have on how we might be involved. And don't be bashful."

Jimmy Carter takes a well-deserved break from all that hammering.

(Photo by Julie Lopez)

I wasn't. And the rest has been chronicled in many a headline and television news report—so much so that Jimmy Carter has become connected with Habitat for Humanity in the country's public consciousness.

I knew President Carter to be a talented carpenter, and soon he was putting those skills to work before the nation's eyes, inspiring in the process many more national figures to do the same. Each year since 1984, he has given time for what we call the Jimmy Carter Work Project, creating annual excitement and exposure that has mushroomed Habitat volunteerism and fund-raising—and building some solid houses and new communities of hope and pride in the process.

The media loves what Jimmy Carter is doing. A former president is spending his time, not in luxury in some heavily-guarded and plush enclave, not at fancy hotels and jet-set parties, but building houses for *and with* people who need them.

In 1994, Habitat for Humanity hit close to home for him. Through Habitat, President Carter had the opportunity to come to the aid of his former nanny. Seventy-seven-year-old Annie Mae Rhodes who had worked for the Carter family for twenty-two years lost her house in the 1994 summer flood that hit southern Georgia tragically hard. Annie Mae had been very close to the Carter family, even to the point of holding President Carter's father in her arms when he died. As the years passed, she moved away to take care of an invalid brother in Albany, Georgia. As President Carter said in an Associated Press story about her, "She is a person whom I have loved since I was a young boy. She means a lot to us. She wasn't even going to let us know she was in trouble." In fact, two Atlanta women, employees of BellSouth Telecommunications who were doing flood relief work, happened to notice this older woman who was helping other people. They soon found out that her house had been damaged beyond repair too, and as they were helping her sort through her damaged belongings, they happened to see some pictures of the president and the Carter extended family. So they asked her about it. "Oh, I used to work for the Carters," she said. *Does he know about your situation,* they asked? "Probably not," she replied. "He's too busy to be concerned with something like that." So one of them wrote to President Carter about Annie Mae's housing needs.

Linda and I go to the same church as the Carters. One morning during his Sunday school hour, President Carter was telling the group about Annie Mae Rhodes and next thing I knew, he turned to me and asked, "Can the local Habitat affiliate help her?"

I contacted the Albany affiliate and asked them to help. Soon, plans were underway for a new home for Annie Mae Rhodes. The BellSouth Company and their Telephone Pioneers, a group made up of BellSouth's retired employees, agreed to sponsor the house, including funding and volunteers. The Carters found time to significantly help with both the demolition of the old flooded house and the building of the new one. By December, Annie Mae Rhodes' new Habitat house was finished and ready for her to move in. Jimmy Carter was there to hand her the keys in a moving dedication service.

This is one of many memorable times we've experienced with the Carters over the years of working together in Habitat for Humanity. I remember very well, for example, a couple of interesting moments.

I vividly recall the very first time Jimmy Carter came to give us a day's work as a volunteer on one of our construction crews in Americus. At one point, when the crew was lifting a set of framing into place, it slipped and began to topple right toward President Carter. One of the Secret Service men quickly jumped between him and the falling wall, grabbing it just in time to stave off serious injury. Later, one of the workmen fired a little gun that shoots a concrete nail through the wood framing into the concrete floor. The BANG! of the gun brought the Secret Service men to full alert, and we all laughed more than a little nervously. Otherwise, the day was a huge success, paving the way for all that followed.

I'll never forget the excitement—the astonishment, really—of President Carter's hands-on participation in what became the first Jimmy Carter Work Project. It was a Habitat project already under renovation on East Sixth Street in New York City, a six-story tenement being gutted and slowly transformed. Earlier, he had dropped by the New York City site at our invitation while in town for a speaking engagement, and was promptly led up five flights of a temporary wooden staircase completed two days earlier. "Let Millard know if there's anything I can do to help you," he told the director of the project, Rob DeRocker.

Rob replied quickly: "Why don't you come back with a group from your church for a work week?"

Soon, that was exactly what happened. We began to make plans for this extraordinary work party. Volunteers were recruited, a bus chartered, and arrangements made to stay at Metro Baptist Church where we would be sleeping on cots during the work week.

As word leaked out about the planned event, phones began to ring. The media had lots of questions:

"Is President Carter really going to ride on the bus all the way to New York?"

"Is it true he intends to sleep in a bunk bed at Metro Baptist Church?"

"Is he actually planning to do physical work on the building?"

The press reaction ranged from skeptical to astonished to genuinely impressed.

My favorite question to President Carter, though, was asked by a reporter at a press conference on the first day of the work week: "Isn't it unusual for a former vice president to be involved in something like this?"

President Carter's response? "Not having been a vice president, I don't feel I can answer that question." There were great peals of laughter, and then the President added, "That question, I suppose, only goes to show how fleeting fame is."

I'll never forget the crowds that gathered outside on the street in front of the building for that first Jimmy Carter Work Project, chanting "Jimmy! Jimmy! Jimmy!" each time they saw a glimpse of the former president working above. "The Today Show" and "Good Morning America" were there to beam it to the rest of the country, and so many calls came in to the New York Habitat office that we had to send two volunteers to the offices to help with the phones. The president of the New York District Council of the United Brotherhood of Carpenters and Joiners of America came to the building to present a check for five hundred dollars and a gold union card to President Carter, as well as pledging material and volunteer work from some of their members. And that was just the beginning of professional and personal responses and offerings. A touching example was an elderly man who lived in the once-elegant building seventy-eight years earlier calling to donate one thousand dollars.

As President Carter wrote about their work in New York in a *House & Garden* magazine article:

> "Rosalynn and I have never had a more memorable and fulfilling experience than the work camps we led to the Lower East Side in Manhattan. The work was difficult, dirty, and sometimes even dangerous, but every moment was packed with a feeling of gratitude that we could be part of the project."

Each year since that first work project in 1984, President Carter has led a week-long blitz building project. Linda and I have been with the Carters every year. We returned to New York in 1985, went to Chicago in '86, to Charlotte, North Carolina in '87, and to Philadelphia and Atlanta in '88. Milwaukee was the scene of the 1989 Project, Tijuana, Mexico and San Diego, California in '90, Miami, Florida in '91, Washington, D.C. in '92, Winnipeg, Manitoba and Kitchener, Ontario Canada in '93, Eagle Butte, South Dakota in '94 and in 1995 Los Angeles.

Eagle Butte was an unusually significant Jimmy Carter Work Project experience. On July 18–25 at the Cheyenne River Sioux Indian Reservation, more than fifteen hundred volunteers from forty-eight states and five countries joined with thirty Lakota Sioux families from Eagle Butte to build a community. Okiciyapi Tipi is the name the local Habitat affiliate gave itself. Loosely translated, the Lakota words mean "helping each other build houses." And that's exactly what our group headed by Jimmy Carter did that year. The affiliate was brand-new, so the blitz was a major challenge. Still we saw this as an opportunity to break into another segment of our society and an answer to our great desire to work on Indian reservations across the country.

By doing a dramatic event like a Jimmy Carter Work Project on the reservation, we knew that Habitat's work would become known in Native American circles. Leaders from several Indian reservations came to Eagle Butte to meet with President Carter. At the beginning of the week a big pow-wow was held to kick off the work with lots of pageantry, including traditional Indian dress along with dancing and drumming.

They had set up three big tipis at the edge of the building site and all the leaders from the various tribes invited us to sit with them in a

(Photo by Julie Lopez)

The Carters were honored during the huge Pow-Wow at the Cheyenne River Sioux Indian Reservation in Eagle Butte, South Dakota.

big circle on buffalo hides and smoke a peace pipe with them, which we did. Later, at the nearby ceremonial grounds, a Lakota ceremony took place honoring President Carter and me. We were each presented an eagle feather which the leaders proceeded to tie into our hair on the back of our heads. (The crowd was informed of the seriousness of this ceremony and people were asked not to take pictures.) We were then given Lakota names. President Carter's was "Wa-wi-hakta," or "One who cares for the people." Mine was "Ta Tipi Waste Kaga," which means "Good house maker." And all three thousand people who attended the event lined up to shake our hands. It was quite a night.

The Eagle Butte project was the first blitz build to take place on a reservation. Austin Keith, Habitat's director of our American Indian Initiative and a Lakota Sioux, saw the effort as historic and significant for special reasons. "It's about reconciliation," he explained, a feeling we all wanted to be true as we sensed that an important new Habitat work was being launched.

The majority of volunteers slept in six hundred two-person dome tents at the local elementary school. Others camped in their own recreational vehicles at the pow-wow grounds. Breakfast was served in the elementary school cafeteria; then volunteers boarded local school buses for the mile-long ride to the work site. With the exception of a tipi instead of a tent to sleep in, the accommodations for President and Mrs. Carter were no different than the others.

It was hot. It was windy. Then it turned cold. One day rain and hail slowed down progress. Many volunteers worked until midnight to keep the houses on schedule.

I had invited NBC-television news anchor Tom Brokaw to build with us since he was a native South Dakotan, and he did. He worked along with the Carters on Emanuel and Cheryl Red Bear's house for two days. Then while visiting on "The David Letterman Show" later that year, he talked about the experience. Being a cynical reporter, he said, made him ready to find the faults of Habitat for Humanity while there, but he found none. Then he went on to express praise and appreciation, giving us wonderful, free, and unexpected national exposure.

At the end of the week, Housing and Urban Development (HUD) Secretary Henry Cisneros paid a visit to the work site, and pitched in on several houses.

(Photo by Julie Lopez)

Tom Brokaw, a native of South Dakota, helps raise walls at the 1994 Jimmy Carter Work Project in Eagle Butte.

Two groups of cyclists pedaled in from Minneapolis/St. Paul, Minnesota (five hundred miles), and from Winnipeg, Manitoba, Canada (seven hundred miles). The cyclists were met by Lakota runners on Sunday afternoon and escorted into town with an honor run.

Okiciyapi Tipi Habitat for Humanity also extended a special invitation to their proposed tithe affiliate, the Tarahumara indigenous people of northern Mexico. Along with a small contingency of Hahnu, another indigenous Mexican Indian tribe from central Mexico, they helped on the site for the whole week. As Felicitas Cordonas from Chihuahua said, "Despite the weight of being peoples from so far apart, we can identify with brothers."

Since Eagle Butte, word about Habitat has been spreading to other Indian reservations in South Dakota and other states. Inquiries have come in to the offices of the American Indian Initiative in Sioux Falls from reservations in Montana, Wyoming, California, North Dakota, and Utah. This is how Habitat spreads, and it's terrific to watch.

The brand new Eagle Butte community that came into being in that one week is situated in roughly a horseshoe shape with a central "hochoka," or common area, in the middle where the children's playground is located. The playground, by the way, has already been named: Tomahawk Park— in honor of John Tomahawk, a local resident who assisted virtually every family with their sweat equity requirements in the weeks leading up to the Jimmy Carter Work Project. The new Habitat homeowners were already making plans to add a basketball court and soccer field.

"The Lakota people are impressed by you," said Keith to the volunteers sitting in the bleachers along with the Carters and me during the Habitation celebration on the last night.

"I cannot thank you enough for what you have done here this week," added Tribal Chairman Gregg Bourland. "What you have done for my people is too great. You have done what the Bible says, 'Love one another.' You have done that. You have loved my people."[1]

As we gained more media exposure, as more and more people learned what Habitat was all about, we began to attract other well-known people with the clout and the heart to make their own impact for this crazy idea called Habitat for Humanity.

To name a few:

- Bill and Hillary Clinton, Al and Tipper Gore, and their children worked on a Habitat house in Atlanta.

- Country singer Reba McEntire sponsored a house, then another one.

- Paul Newman continues to be a wonderful supporter contributing generous amounts each year from his "Newman's Own" business, and he personally helped build Habitat houses in Lexington, Kentucky.

- Author and humorist Garrison Keillor has contributed and has performed a benefit concert.

- Former President Gerald Ford serves on our board of advisors.

- Speaker of the House Newt Gingrich has been spotted wearing a Habitat lapel pin, and he, his staff, and "Friends of Newt" sponsored a Habitat house in his home county of Cobb in Georgia. The project was called "Building with Newt."

- Former Congressman and Secretary of Housing and Urban Development Jack Kemp has been an outspoken advocate for Habitat, and has served as a member of our board of directors as well as hammering some nails.

- World Heavyweight Boxing Champion Evander Holyfield appeared in a "Home Improvement" television episode about Habitat for Humanity.

- Bob Hope, who has given generously to Habitat over the years, swung a hammer once in the Jimmy Carter Work Project in Charlotte—and bent the nail.

- Miss America Kimberly Aiken was a hard worker during the 1994 Super Bowl XXVIII Blitz Build in Atlanta.

- National League Football players Billy Joe Tolliver, Mike Haynes, Glyn Milburn, John Elway, Eric Turner, and Warren Moon pulled their impressive weight on the same Super Bowl Blitz Build.

- For the second Super Bowl Blitz Build, Miami's Super Bowl XXIX, professional football players Neil Smith, Calvin Williams, Glyn Milburn, and Eric Turner worked on five Miami-area houses.

- Singer Amy Grant has begun to feature the Habitat for Humanity logo on her concert posters and to talk about Habitat during her appearances in a wonderful partnership. During her 1995 tour she talked about Habitat for Humanity in connection with one of her songs called "Helping Hand," accompanied by a video of Amy at a Habitat building site. Also, as spokesperson for the Target Store chain, a corporation committed to building a Habitat house for every new store it opens, she is giving generously toward those new houses. Amy is a terrific partner who is making a strategic difference in exposing Habitat's mission to her young fans in a unique and effective way.

Habitat itself has even been a television "star"—shining for one night, anyway, in March 1994 on TV's top-rated show of the year. ABC's "Home Improvement" starring Tim Allen filmed an episode concerning Habitat for Humanity during the 1994 Super Bowl Blitz Build. The plot line went like this: NFL football players along with the former heavy-weight boxing champion of the world were building a Habitat house next door to one being built totally by women, including Miss America. Competition was soon underway to see who could build the better house—the women or the men. Of course, people began falling through the floors of the men's house while the women's house was perfect. In the end, President Carter appeared in a cameo role, announcing that he was proud of the women but that a crew was still trying to repair the house the big bruisers had tried to build—saying it all, of course, with a straight face.

The list goes on: Willie Nelson, Ben Vereen, Ken Medema, Richie Havens, Gregory Hines, The Indigo Girls, Margaret Becker, Buddy Greene, and Jane Fonda are more of the many national figures who've given time and their celebrity status to Habitat's cause. While their

(Photo by Julie Lopez)

Tim Allen (left) and the crew of ABC-TV's "Home Improvement" present a check for $10,000 to Habitat following the taping of a special episode of the show about Habitat for Humanity.

famous faces have brought wonderful publicity for Habitat, many of these well-known figures also have been a lot of fun when they've come to help us actually build a house or do a benefit performance.

Bob Hope was one of the first celebrities to come to a building site. Earlier, I mentioned the benefit he did for the Charlotte, North Carolina Jimmy Carter Work Project, and that he bent the nail he hammered. The whole story, though, is funnier still. When he came on site that afternoon, our folks had a Habitat tee shirt and hat ready for him, as well as a nail apron and a hammer. Unknown to Bob, we had replaced the nails in the apron with a lot of golf tees. We directed him to a window that was being installed. We asked him to drive a nail into one of the boards around the window. He reached into his apron for a nail, and instead pulled out a handful of the tees. Everyone exploded in laughter. When the crowd quieted down, we gave him a real nail. He bent it. We gave him another nail. He bent that one too. He bent every nail he tried to put in. That evening, though, he gave the benefit, and the only thing *bent* about it was the audience—often bent over in hilarious laughter.

Another humorous episode occurred when Jack Kemp was on the work site of the Super Bowl Blitz Build in Atlanta. He was given the job of putting up a banister on a porch, which was being screwed instead of nailed. Someone handed him a screw gun, and the cameras began to roll. However, there seemed to be a problem. Jack kept trying to screw in the screw, but the harder he pushed, the more the screw wobbled and refused to go in. You could tell he was rather embarrassed by the ordeal. He handed the gun to me and asked me to take a look at it. I immediately saw the problem. Someone had flipped the switch which made the screw gun screw backward instead of forward.

So, without Jack seeing me, I flipped the switch back the correct way and quickly screwed a screw right in, shrugging as if nothing was wrong at all. Jack and everyone else looked amazed. That's when I confessed, and even Jack laughed. He took the gun away from me and quickly screwed in a few for the cameras.

Paul Newman is one of Habitat's most generous partners. He came to Lexington, Kentucky in the summer of 1991 to be a part of a fifteen-house blitz build. I was there with him on the last afternoon, and after

(Photo by Chris McGranahan)

Solving the "mystery of the reversing screw gun," Millard Fuller (left) steps in to help Jack Kemp (center) during the 1994 Super Bowl Blitz Build.

working for awhile, we went around from house to house for photographs. I found out what it was like to be a movie idol, watching everyone's reaction to his famous face. But I also enjoyed how he reacted to the crowd. For instance, as we walked up to one house with all of the assembled volunteers out front, a lady rushed forward and gushed, "Mr. Newman, would you please take off your sunglasses? I want to see your eyes!"

Without missing a beat, he retorted, "I would like to, but if I take my sunglasses off, my pants will fall down." The lady just melted back into the crowd.

Sometimes we meet these people in the strangest ways. During the August 1992 presidential campaign, candidate Bill Clinton and his family were set to work on a Habitat for Humanity house in Atlanta. The work was scheduled for a Monday, and Linda and I as well as our youngest daughter Georgia were going to join them. Afterward, we planned to go to Florida for a few days of vacation with Georgia before she left to study for a year in France. A week before the blitz build, I received a call from Bill Clinton's office, saying that they were changing the day he'd be there—from Monday to Wednesday. Since I already had

Newt Gingrich nails on siding on a house sponsored by "Friends of Newt" in Cobb County, Georgia.

(Photo by Doug Woods)

(Photo by Julie Lopez)

Actor Paul Newman deftly handles a paint brush at a Habitat blitz build in Lexington, Kentucky.

Actress Jane Fonda hammers a nail at the 20/20,000 Blitz Build in Americus in 1993.

(Photo by Julie Lopez)

(Photo by Kimberly Prenda)

Amy Grant joins new homeowner Theresa Hathaway and her sons Troy (left) and Eric for Christmas dedication of their Habitat house.

promised that time to my daughter Georgia, I informed Bill Clinton's office that we would not be there. I knew that President Carter would be working with the Clintons, so I felt my presence was not essential.

But then, while headed to the cabin of a friend on Grayton Beach near Destin, Florida where we would be vacationing, I read in the local paper that Senator Al Gore was also vacationing in Destin with his family that week. I decided I'd try to contact Senator Gore to see if he was planning to work with the Clintons in Atlanta. The next morning, Linda and I got up early and went for a walk on the beach. We hadn't been walking for very long when four people jogged by.

Linda said, "Those two men running behind the others look like Secret Service agents."

I said, "They are—and that's Al Gore."

Deciding quickly that we'd catch them and take advantage of the opportunity to talk, we broke into a trot. Thankfully, they soon turned around and started jogging back toward us, so we went right up to them. Senator Gore looked surprised at first, but then knew right away who I was. He explained that he knew what Habitat for Humanity was all about, and he informed us he and his family were going to fly to Atlanta in their plane to work on the blitz build along with the Clintons, then return to Destin Wednesday afternoon. Would I like to come along? After talking it over with Georgia and Linda, I said "Yes," and the next day I was in Atlanta helping to build a house with the Clintons, the Gores, and the Carters.

By the way, when Bill Clinton was inaugurated, he invited the home-owner of that house, Michelle Miller—with whom he had worked on the project—to attend the inauguration. A nice gown was provided for her and all her expenses were paid by the Inaugural Committee to attend the festivities surrounding the inauguration. Later she was asked to be a part of "Faces of Hope"—a meeting of people whom President Clinton and Vice President Gore had met during the campaign and who had particularly impressed them.

The list of celebrities and well-known figures who have swung a hammer for Habitat (or the financial equivalent) keeps growing. The exposure given the cause by such well-known people to help end poverty housing in the world has been inestimable.

For people blessed with such visible influence and affluence, what better way to use those gifts than by helping the "invisible" of our country and around the world have a simple, decent place to live?

(Photo by Kimberly Prenda)

The Clintons, Gores, Carters, and Millard Fuller during a joyous moment at a Habitat construction site in Atlanta.

CHAPTER FIVE

What Difference
Does a House Make?

Changing Lives, One Family at a Time

WHAT HAPPENS TO the people who move into Habitat houses? Probably more than any other question, I'm asked how a house could change the lives of the people who live in it. Well, let me tell you just a few of the stories of changed lives within Habitat walls. I'll start by sharing how people *feel* about getting a new Habitat house. I do so because an explosion of appreciation, love, and hope in the life of a family is the beginning of new and better things.

Listen to eight-year-old Brandie Moore and her six-year-old sister April as they express their sentiments about their new Habitat house in Pensacola, Florida. Brandie read the following letter at the dedication of their house on Sunday afternoon, February 19, 1995:

Dear Habitat,

Thank you for our beautiful house. We really love living in it. It is the most beautiful in the whole world. I don't know how you built it, but you did—and you did a wonderful and fantastic job on our beautiful house. We really, really, really, really enjoy living in it. We don't know how to thank you, but thank you very, very, very much for our beautiful, wonderful, and most fantastic house. It seems like you've been doing it for years and years and years. I have never ever in my whole life seen somebody doing something so beautiful and so fast without making one little tinsey, bitty, tiny mistake. We really, really, really appreciate it. Thank you very, very much.

Brandie and April

Another grateful child was ten-year-old Charlie. He and his family lived in a very inadequate rented house in Olympia, Washington. Previously, the family had lived in their car. One day they heard about Habitat for Humanity. An application was filled out and the family waited several weeks for an answer. Finally, it came. A small delegation from the Family Selection Committee went to their house and announced to the family that they had been chosen to receive a Habitat house.

Immediately, Charlie began jumping up and down, shouting, "We won! We won! We won!"

Charlie helped build his new house—*and* many forts and a great tree house with scrap lumber from the construction site.

In his previous school, Charlie was in a class for slow learners. When the house was finished, the family moved in and Charlie started attending his new school, which was in a different district. Somehow, his school records did not get properly transferred so Charlie was put in a regular track fourth-grade class.

Several months passed. Charlie became a solid "B" student. Then, at a conference for teachers held in the city, his former teacher met his new teacher. As they talked about Charlie, both were amazed. It seems that Charlie had been so worried about his living situation, and especially fearful of having to move back into a car, that he couldn't concentrate on his school work. A decent house, along with all the love that comes with it, literally *liberated* his mind to learn!

A truly heartwarming expression of appreciation and a testimony of what a difference a Habitat house can make came in a letter to Linda and me from Amy Browne, mother of the first homeowner family in the Penn-York Habitat for Humanity affiliate in Sayre, Pennsylvania. In a letter dated November 13, 1994, she wrote:

We are homeowners that you have rescued from poverty housing.

We received our new home on October 16, 1993. The next morning we woke up with lots of unpacking to do—but we were warm. We've been here for thirteen months and we love it. Our youngest child was very sick with chronic asthma. He was on daily medication including breathing treatments and steroids. He was in the hospital a lot. He was very sick before we moved in. Now he is off all medicines and you would never know just how sick he was before. Little Timmy is yet another life you've saved, and for that we thank you.

I strongly believe in Habitat. I've caught the vision. I am on the Family Selection Committee, so I can help other families feel as blessed as we do. I am also our affiliate's Volunteer Coordinator, a job I've had since March of '94. I have personally grown a lot since we became the affiliate's first partner family. I used to be very quiet, and public speaking seemed unthinkable. On September 17, 1994, I led a workshop on volunteering. I also brought up an idea to do a big fundraiser. My idea was taken seriously and on December 4, we are doing a big concert (country music) and I am a speaker. I volunteer a lot of time to our local affiliate—usually five to ten hours a week.

I often wish that I could meet you and Linda, just to give you a hug and say "thanks" from the bottom of my heart.

God bless,

Todd and Amy Browne
Amber, Alex, and Timothy

Amy got her chance to meet Linda and me at the Mid-Atlantic Habitat Regional meeting which was held in Harrisonburg, Pennsylvania on the weekend of May 5, 1995. Her letter was read by Associate Director Robin Monaghan at the opening session of the annual Habitat conference. The whole family was called up to the stage. Linda and I hugged them and then posed for numerous pictures as the hundreds of people at the event cheered and clapped. Timmy, especially, was radiant and an absolute picture of health.

When the picture taking and hugging ended, the family started back to their seats. As they descended from the stage, little Timmy yelled out so that everyone could hear, "I *like* this job!"

For some—hope being the powerful force it is—a house can mean health, even mental health. That was the story for Valerie Estes MatoWanbliMani (Walking Eagle Bear) when she moved into her new Habitat house built during the 1994 Jimmy Carter Work Project at Eagle Butte, South Dakota. Her house was one of the thirty blitz-built on the Cheyenne River Sioux Indian Reservation. Valerie, the mother of four children, was diagnosed as clinically depressed in 1990; she'd been the victim of physical and sexual abuse as a child and the guilt, shame, and repressed anger from those traumatic episodes brewed in her for many years until finally she was all but paralyzed with depression. Since the age of twelve, she'd felt a pervasive sense of utter hopelessness. Finally as an adult, she found herself hardly able to get off the couch much of the time.

An uncle encouraged her to apply for one of the Habitat houses to be built on the reservation. He had been to the 1993 Jimmy Carter Work Project in Winnipeg and was excited by what he saw. He told Valerie that she probably would never have an opportunity like this again. When Valerie saw an announcement on the local cable channel about a Habitat meeting, she knew she should go. It was all she could do, though, to get off the couch and put her shoes on and go down to the Habitat office. "I didn't even comb my hair," she recalls. "I went over there looking like a ragamuffin. And the real reason I went to the Habitat office that day was because I wanted to break up my day. I remember thinking, 'Okay, I did *one living thing* today.'"

Valerie filled out her application, handed it in, and left—before the orientation meeting was over. She had to get away from all the people. Her application was approved. But she knew she was going to have a hard time meeting the sweat equity requirement, due to low energy levels from her clinical depression. Fortunately, the construction supervisor tuned into Valerie's limitations and gave her very specific tasks to do—tasks Valerie could successfully complete.

All was in order by the time the Jimmy Carter Work Project began. But the thought of being around all the people who would be coming to the work project did nothing but raise her fears. She was afraid . . . afraid to join in and afraid of being pushed to the sidelines and ignored in the flurry of activity. Yet she was taken care of. "Habitat just knows the

(Photo by Julie Lopez)

Valerie Estes works on her Habitat house on the Cheyenne River Sioux Indian Reservation in Eagle Butte, South Dakota.

right things to do," Valerie said, referring to the "buddy" she was assigned during the week of house-building. "Habitat gathered us [homeowner families] up like a bunch of chickens and paired us up. That was the first thing Habitat did to stop my fear."

The group prayed before they began. Valerie started crying. "I just released all my junk," she explained. Best of all, Valerie felt hopeful about life, and she believed the Eagle Butte houses also had the same effect on her neighbors. "They're a source of healing for our people, for our community."

All of the new homeowners are showing a pride never seen before on the reservation when it comes to housing. Their new houses are building a sense of community. When the children's playground was vandalized, the homeowners' association called a meeting, set an evening curfew, and sandpapered the graffiti off the wood themselves.

"There is a long list of programs that haven't worked on the reservations. The Jimmy Carter Work Project has brought hope to our people in the form of thirty houses," says Austin Keith, director of Habitat's American Indian Initiative. "It has established relationships between the affiliate and other agencies such as the Indian Health Service hospital which funded the mile-long waterline to the site, the rural electric company, and the tribal leadership there . . . It shows other tribes that Habitat for Humanity can work in a reservation setting."

Time and again we've seen how good housing truly has the power to transform whole neighborhoods in the same way it changes individuals and families. Sometimes the change is financial.

The Habitat for Humanity affiliate in Dallas, Texas is credited with turning around the East Garrett Park neighborhood and actually increasing

Austin Keith, director of Habitat's American Indian Initiative, at the work site in Eagle Butte, South Dakota.

(Habitat for Humanity file photo)

property values. In East Garrett Park, Habitat built or rehabilitated more than 75 percent of the homes. Property values increased almost 100 percent. Houses that were once valued at $12,000–$18,000 are now appraised at more than $30,000.

In the Midtown area of Jackson, Mississippi, Catherine Thomas has lived on Nearview Street for eighteen years. During that time she has seen her neighborhood, located within one mile of the state capitol, deteriorate drastically. Abandoned homes with overgrown lots became as much a part of living in Midtown as the ever-present crack dealer on the corner. Often, she would awaken to the sound of gunshots instead of her alarm clock. She prayed for relief. Then one day she saw workers clearing land near her home and went to investigate. "When they told me who they were, I said, 'Bless you, Jesus—Habitat is here.'"

Since Metro Jackson Habitat for Humanity made a commitment to focus its building in the Midtown area, the effect on the neighborhood has been profound. Residents report that drug dealers left and pride returned. City officials were delighted to see Habitat concentrate their commitment and investment there too. "When Habitat started talking about what they were going to do, we were overjoyed," remembers Phil Harwick, who was director of Jackson's development and planning department in 1993. By 1995, Metro Jackson Habitat for Humanity had pumped more than one million dollars into Midtown, with funding coming from sponsors and individuals. "This has a momentum all its own, like a train that everyone wants to climb on. People are inspired because they finally see someone taking action."

Now, where there were once boarded-up shacks and crack houses, there are children playing amid a profusion of flowers. In two separate blocks of Midtown, twenty-eight houses have been reclaimed or built new. Current plans call for at least sixty Habitat homes in the area. The development is right on schedule, and Catherine Thomas now hears the sounds of hammers and saws instead of gunfire and police sirens—the sound of a neighborhood coming back to life.[1]

Ermon Lature, president of Nashville Area Habitat for Humanity, wrote in their Fall 1994 newsletter, *Hammer to Nail,* about the changes in Habitat neighborhoods and in the people, especially the children:

> "Yards are cut and cleaned up, houses are painted. Pride is contagious . . . kids learn better if they live in a drug-free neighborhood. Two small Nashville boys are taken from a dangerous environment and their teachers are amazed at the change in the confidence of both. Their grandmother says the confidence comes from the disappearance of constant fear in their lives. They go home to a comfortable house that has room enough for a quiet place to study and do homework. (i.e. A police officer investigated the light on in a nearly completed Habitat house and discovered that the 'intruder' was the teenage daughter of the soon-to-be owner. She was studying in 'her' room.)"

Often, a Habitat house changes attitudes, brings people together, and equips them for new and better opportunities in life.

Habitat homeowner Rosie Simmons of Chicago wrote this about her changes:

Through Habitat, I now know how to put on a door knob. I can fix a hole in the wall. I am getting ready to return to school, and I am looking forward to starting a new job—one that will provide more security and allow me to spend more time at home with my children. My children can now see life from a different view. Habitat has given me hope. I won't stop here; I will continue to move forward and I will continue to love Habitat and work in any way I can. I thank God for Habitat, that 'giant eraser' that continues to erase the lines that separate black from white, rich from poor, educated from uneducated, and one denomination from another.

Rosie, incidentally, got that new job—with a prestigious bank in downtown Chicago. Hers is a wonderful story of a renewed life, with promise being fulfilled.

Time after time we see people move into Habitat houses and go back to school, enter college, do all sorts of things they never dreamed were within their reach before they had the enveloping hope of a simple, decent place to live. And the effect on the children of these families is often dramatic. Joanne Waters who was living in a garage with her children in northern California, now lives in her Habitat house. One of the first things she will tell you about is her son's straight A's.

Tim and Kathy Richardson know the difference a house can make in the lives of children. They and their five children were struggling to make ends meet on an annual income of seven thousand dollars in the Appalachian Mountains of Tennessee. "We had moved three times in less than a year looking for good jobs, but area industries failed," Kathy explained. They ended up in a two-bedroom mobile home. A local manufacturer's donation of a complete framing package for a five-bedroom log house to the local Habitat affiliate made it possible for the affiliate to build an affordable house large enough for the Richardson family. Soon, they were living in their new Habitat house.

"The kids have thrived," Kathy reports. "It gave my children the kind of stability all children need. It gave them a home to be proud of." Her oldest, now twenty, has joined the navy, and her eighteen-year-old is in college. Two others are in high school and the youngest is in eighth grade. And what about the house? The family has been in it for a decade. Kathy speaks without equivocation, "I see this house being

(Habitat for Humanity file photo)

Habitat families quickly settled into their new homes following the 1988 Jimmy Carter Work Project in Atlanta, Georgia.

passed on for one hundred years. It's too much of a dream come true to ever let it go."[2]

A recent survey of forty Habitat homeowners from the Twin Cities Habitat for Humanity affiliate in Minneapolis/St. Paul explored the positive impact of homeownership among their homeowners. The survey found that improvement in education, health, financial stability, and/or decreased family conflict were the positive results of living in a Habitat house.

As Jimmy Carter explained in a speech, "Drugs, crime, education, health care, and dreams for the future don't seem to be directly related to housing, but you know they are. This past summer Rosalynn and I led a group of workers in Philadelphia. . . . One of the most vivid things we learned was taught to us by a woman who had moved into a Habitat house shortly before we arrived. She pointed out that she had children, including some teenage boys who were a constant source of concern to her. When night came, she never knew where they were. She knew they were running around in a crowd that was often in trouble—even being imprisoned on occasion. She could see her children going to a life of crime. Then she got a Habitat house, and all of a sudden her boys started coming home and they brought their friends home with them. And they told their mama, 'Before we got this house, we were ashamed to let any of our friends know where we lived.'

"I've talked to Habitat mamas and daddies who didn't finish high school themselves—who never thought about finishing high school. *Their* parents didn't finish high school. Then just a few days after moving into a Habitat house, sometimes even when they were moving in, they began to talk about which college their children were going to attend. So, does housing have anything to do with crime? With drugs? With education? With ambition? With dreams? With happiness? I think so."

Sometimes the changes can be seen almost instantaneously.

I remember a letter sent to me by Robert K. Whitford, a professor at Purdue University who had helped organize the Habitat affiliate in Lafayette, Indiana. "In a sense, redemption is occurring in front of our eyes," he wrote. "The change in our first family (a single-parent family with three teenage boys) is astonishing. Janie, the mother, is like a new person—brighter, cheerier, dressing and carrying herself more confidently. She no longer has to carry water four miles because the pipes are frozen or live huddled up in two rooms of a dilapidated ten-room farmhouse. She seems to have renewed faith. Her three teenage sons also are behaving very differently. Tommy, the eldest, took on the drafting of the house plans by working after school with his drafting instructor. This from a boy whose interest in school had always been minimal. The whole family has been on the site working, and their attitude has been extremely infectious for the volunteers."

It's a dynamic I love to see. Helping people help themselves into their own homes does something that goes beyond just giving shelter. It does something for people on the inside. It's an intangible quality of hope that so many in our society don't have, the quality without which a person feels like a "loser" in life. All they may have known is loss. For many, a Habitat house is the first real victory of their lives and it can be transforming.

One such moment of victory stands out in my mind from as far back as 1984. We were dedicating a new Habitat house in Americus for Diane Ellis. Diane and her family had moved out of an unpainted, uninsulated shack which Diane said was so cold in the winter they had to go outside to get warm. There was a single spigot near the back door for water. As Habitat people and Diane's friends and neighbors crowded into her yard for the dedication service, she stepped to the microphone.

"I suppose all of you want to know how I feel about this new house," she said quietly. "Well, I'll tell you."

She took a step backwards and began to jump up and down yelling, "Yippee! Yippee! Yippee!" She waved her arms and kept right on yelling the same word over and over: "Yippee! Yippee! Yippee!" Finally she stopped. Everyone was laughing. But then, as if she'd only stopped to catch her breath, she started right up again, this time shouting even louder: "Yippee! Yippee! Yippee!" She stopped again, and this time the laughter was softer because she immediately started again: "Yippee! Yippee! Yippee!" When Diane finally stopped, exhausted but joyous, eyes filled with tears, everyone in the yard was beginning to cry too. It was a powerful and magic moment. We all stood, quietly moved by the experience for a few minutes more before we could resume the dedication ceremonies.

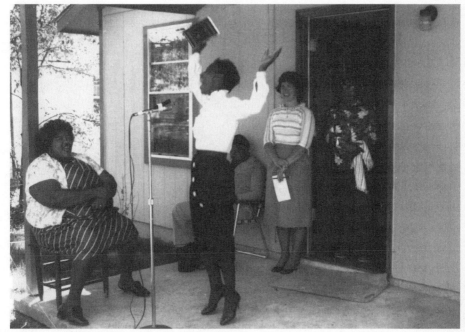

(Habitat for Humanity file photo)

"Yippee, Yippee!" shouts Diane Ellis at the dedication of her Habitat house.

A similar outburst of excitement about a new Habitat house occurred more recently, in late 1994, on the other side of the world in the town of Kasane, Botswana, in southern Africa. Habitat's International Partner Amy Sobota wrote about the event in her newsletter:

> "After making his first house payment, Sechoni proudly received his keys and went over to inspect his new Habitat house. He opened the front door and went in. A few minutes later, we could see him through the window jumping up and down with a joy that couldn't be expressed any other way."

Another explosion of exuberance came from a ten-year-old boy named Bobby. His family received a Habitat house in Grand Junction, Colorado in early 1994. I was in Grand Junction soon after the family moved into their new house and had the privilege of meeting Bobby.

His mother was the custodian of one of the local churches. On the Sunday after they moved into their new house, the family went to the early Sunday morning worship service, as was their custom. They sat in their usual place, toward the back of the sanctuary.

Since the family regularly attended church, Bobby knew the order of the service and he knew specifically that there were a few moments of silence at one particular point in the service. So, at that precise moment, he jumped up on the pew and shouted out, "Hey, everybody! We moved into our new Habitat house this past week and we sure do like it and I want to thank everybody!" And then he sat down.

At the conclusion of the service, Bobby's family returned home. But not Bobby. He stayed for the second service, and at the same point in that service he once again jumped up on the pew and cried out, "Hey, everybody! We moved into our new Habitat house this past week and we sure do like it and I want to thank everybody!" Then he sat down again.

No one was left in doubt about the gratitude in Bobby's heart about his new house and no one doubted either that the house would make a positive difference in his life and in the lives of other members of his family.

As the executive director for Fresno, California Habitat for Humanity, Jackie Holmes, put it in PriceCostco Corporation's member magazine article profiling Habitat: "I've seen Habitat's magic work so many times, I don't know if I can put it into words; everyone's working toward a concrete, agreed-upon goal, so you don't focus on your differences. And when you finish a house, you feel like you've changed the world."

Rená Bligen and her family moved out of their tiny trailer into their Habitat house just a year before Hurricane Hugo devastated much of the South Carolina coast in 1989. Their home was undamaged in the storm, while many homes around it were destroyed. Rená Bligen is a social worker with the Department of Social Services for Charleston County, so she sees many troubled families in her work. She investigates and intervenes with families suspected of child abuse or neglect and believes that poor housing is often a factor in the cases.

"Twenty-five percent of the families we encounter are in crisis due to economics," she states. "The families are in substandard housing or homeless shelters." She knows how that feels. Despite her work and her husband's custodial job, if it were not for Habitat, she admits, "We simply could not afford this house." And that ownership has made it possible for Rená to continue her education. She also has begun volunteering with Sea Island Habitat for Humanity's Family Nurture Committee. "I really wanted to give something back," she said.[3]

Life can change at any age, and perhaps a simple, decent place to live becomes more precious as one grows older. In 1982, Viola Allen was a widow with no children maintaining a simple but sufficient lifestyle working for restaurants in Connecticut. Then her elderly mother suffered a stroke and Viola relocated to care for her in her mother's house in Pickens, South Carolina. You really couldn't call it a house. It seemed more like a chicken coop. It had no hot water or toilet, part of the house had a dirt floor, and it contained only a wood stove for cooking and a kerosene heater for warmth. While she struggled to care for her mother in such a place, she noticed Habitat construction going on not far away. She started visiting the work site, helping out, and the affiliate decided that "Miss Viola," as she was affectionately called, should be one of the next homeowners. Soon work began on completely rehabbing the house.

"Miss Viola" contributed sweat equity by keeping the work site clean and by cooking for the work crews. Now a warm, tidy, four-room house with a screen porch stands where the old shack was. That was in 1983. "I'm just as happy as a little pig in the sunshine," Viola says. "I wouldn't take nothing for my little house. Sometimes I just sit out on the porch 'til midnight enjoying it all."

Viola is approaching the end of her mortgage, which she has paid faithfully each month. "The first thing that comes out of my Social Security check is my mortgage payment," she says proudly. "This is the first house I've ever owned. I'll just jump for joy when it's paid off."[4]

John Manavong proves how self-esteem comes with a house. Living on welfare in a two-room apartment with his wife and four children, Manavong had to study in his car for night school. "I could provide my family with clothes and food but not a decent place to live," he told the PriceCostco magazine. "Now I have peace of mind." So much so that he's started his own business making security doors and windows that he often installs into Habitat houses, allowing residents to pay as they're able. That's the community feeling and sense of worth that a simple, decent place to live can nurture.

Nurturing is a big part of Habitat. It can make a dramatic difference. In 1991, after twenty years of struggling with unbearable housing conditions including public housing where her children cried from being scared, where guns, rats, and roaches were the only things that flourished, Imelda Jackson and her family became Habitat homeowners in the Worthdale Forest neighborhood of Raleigh, North Carolina. Not long after, she decided to do something that she could never have imagined doing before Habitat came into her life. She decided to buy and renovate the ramshackle childcare center located in her new community. There was a desperate need for the center. Inadequate plumbing, peeling paint, and a debris-strewn "playground" were just a few of the problems. Only fifteen to twenty children could attend the day-care center and over ninety children needed to be cared for.

She took her idea to the local Habitat affiliate and its leaders agreed to help Jackson make the dream a reality. Some of the Habitat volunteers assisted her in developing a business plan and putting together the legal requirements needed to secure the $35,000 in start-up capital.

Other volunteers helped renovate the building. As Scott Anderson, then executive director of the affiliate, expressed it, "This seemed like a natural extension of what Habitat is all about. There were over ninety-five children in that neighborhood who needed a safe, decent place to be before and after school. Plus, the neighborhood benefits because the building was a hazard and now is a high point, and there is a direct economic impact in the form of jobs."[5]

Habitat *does* change neighborhoods, because neighborhoods are people. The moment people have pride in themselves and their homes, they have a reason to reclaim their neighborhoods.

O. J. Hood is a fine example. According to an article by Ames Alexander in the *Charlotte Observer*, "The ex-marine used to scare people . . . by selling pot, carrying a gun, and beating up his debtors."

Now the people he intimidates are drug dealers in his North Carolina neighborhood. "They move when they see me," Hood is quoted as saying in the article. He told the reporter that homeownership transformed him. Five years ago, he worked alongside a group of volunteers to build his Habitat home. He now counsels other Habitat partners on the fine points of construction and sweat equity. "All these homes have pumped pride into Belmont," Hood said. Shrubs and flowers now stand where litter and weeds once reigned. Now residents don't hide from drug dealers and criminals; they call the police. "If you give a person something to fight for, he'll give you a fight," Hood added. The article told how Hood confronted a drug dealer. "Man, I'd rather be dead in my grave than see you sell poison to my people," Hood told the man. ". . . Bottom line is you're not going to sell drugs in this community." Drug dealers no longer use that street corner.

Habitat-built houses in Belmont have doubled the rate of homeownership in that neighborhood. Habitat for Humanity of Charlotte Executive Director Bert Green believes that alone has helped reduce the crime rate. When people feel a permanent part of the community, they are more inclined to ask what they can do to improve conditions in their community.

One of the reasons the community feeling is so strong is that homeowners expect to stay in their houses and in their neighborhoods for the rest of their lives. Low-income families aren't part of the mobile society that middle America has become. They rarely resell and they just don't leave. They put down roots and stay, and when they have a reason to be proud of where they live, they work hard to stay proud. For the few who do sell for whatever the reason, many affiliates add a first buy-back option for Habitat as part of the agreement of each house sold. So even if the house is sold, odds are the house will be resold to a new Habitat homeowner. Since Habitat is not a charity group, and since homeowners are treated as partners, they are expected to make the monthly payments that go to build other houses. Only a few have defaulted or sold the houses. Habitat homeowners are people who understand the value beyond the money which created the simple, decent place to live which they now call their own.

Of course, Habitat homeowners still have problems. They often are people at risk in society. Habitat works with them in good faith, knowing that owning a home is not the answer to every problem, but one step—often the very first step—toward helping people break out of the cycle of poverty.

Curt and Terri Mason were homeless, living under an Oregon bridge, and more than fifteen thousand dollars in debt when Bend Area Habitat for Humanity selected them as homeowners several years ago. Today, the family is solvent and doing fine. Curt and Terri are serving on the Habitat affiliate's Family Nurture Committee. But maybe the best news of all is that their children are flourishing. In 1990, at the dedication of the family's house, I became fast friends with Jamie, their eight-year-old daughter full of blonde hair and joy. "What do you like most about your house?" I had asked her back then. "Our family will be together and I'm going to have my own room." Five years later, at age thirteen, Jamie is involved in school activities and active in her church youth group as well as an ecumenical discussion group called Open Hearts that meets after school. She says she is "still glad that we all live together."

In Indiana, Lafayette Habitat for Humanity took a chance in 1986 on Mary Stone, a divorced mother of two with a bad credit rating. Since then, Mary has significantly reduced her debt and written a self-help book on handling finances specifically aimed at low-income families.

I would be less than honest if I conveyed the impression that when a Habitat home is finished—after all the struggling with shortages of funds and volunteers and oversupplies of red tape and roadblocks—every family moves into their new home and lives happily ever after. No, in a real way, when the homeowner moves in and the house is complete, the work is nowhere near finished. The nurturing work of Habitat is strategic not only for the families but for Habitat itself. A very important follow-up job every Habitat affiliate has is to make sure house payments keep coming in because every new house depends on this steady income stream. So without those payments coming in, the whole system can break down. Most of our homeowners never miss a payment, but even a small percentage of late payments can slow a local affiliate's work and have a negative impact on the morale of Habitat leaders and volunteers.

Internationally, this is sometimes a hard concept to convey, but creative ways have been used to get the point across. In Kenya, a large sign was placed in front of one house, reading: THIS HOME IS BEING BUILT WITH HOUSE PAYMENTS ONLY. Everyone in that whole area knew without a doubt that if mortgage income to the project slowed down, so did work on that home, and others to follow. In Zaire, the Habitat committee in one city read the names of homeowners in arrears over the local radio station, pointing out that building couldn't continue until people paid their house payments. It worked, peer pressure being the mighty force it is everywhere.

But the best way to ensure regular house payments is through educating the homeowners about the whole Habitat philosophy. Sweat equity is a concept easily understood by any new homeowner. But most Habitat families have never before experienced the complicated demands that go with the responsibility of homeownership.

So to ease the transition, every Habitat affiliate has a committee to work with the new homeowners specifically about such matters. This group makes a strong personal commitment to each family over as many years as may be necessary.

In Chicago, the Uptown Chicago Habitat for Humanity affiliate is solving some serious difficulties in its local area with an effective program that helps families become successful homeowners.

The affiliate's emphasis has been on cooperative homeownership, especially condominiums. Condominium owners need very intensive training that includes information about how to operate a condo association, rules and regulations, and the forming of a board of managers.

Uptown Habitat for Humanity also provides condominium owners with training in basic skills such as financial management, interpersonal skills, and homeownership skills—just as it is provided for homeowners of single-family dwellings. Many people who've never owned a home also have never planted a tree or a garden or fixed a leaky pipe. Often such small handy-man work can seem overwhelming to a new homeowner who knows the responsibility is all theirs and no one else's. The affiliate helps families by teaching them such skills until they feel they can handle these small tasks themselves, like other homeowners do.

Another unique feature of the Uptown Chicago Habitat program is that its Partner Committee, which works with the homeowner families, offers a mentoring program for youth development.

We also try hard to work with other agencies to help change lives. One such story concerns a woman who was a homeless, cocaine-addicted, unemployed mother of three embroiled in an abusive relationship with a man. For years she would use any money she was given or earned for drugs first, food second—often forcing her children to go hungry. One night several years ago, she came to the proverbial end of her tattered rope. She found there was no room in the usual shelters. So she stopped with her children at a bus shelter and settled in for the night. Through that long night, she reviewed her mistakes and decided to start over. She found her way to Cleveland, Ohio's Family Transitional Housing Center and sadly put her children in foster care. Then, with the help of that agency, she kicked her drug habit, severed the abusive relationship, got an apartment, and—once she proved she was serious—reclaimed her children one at a time. She married a friend who encouraged her and now the whole family lives in a Habitat house—a happy ending if I ever heard one.

So what difference does a house make?

Lillie Mae Bownes, an elderly Habitat homeowner in Americus, said it well in a simple statement quoted in a *Reader's Digest* article about Habitat for Humanity:

"I never dreamed I'd have a place like this. It makes us feel like—people."

Joan Jackson of Florence, Alabama expressed her feelings about the difference her family's new Habitat house has made in a poignant poem. I think it sums up the whole matter quite beautifully.

THE BUILDING OF A HOUSE

The building of a house really takes a lot.

Planning and finding the most perfect spot.

The hammers, the nails, the nuts, bolts, and screws,

The wood, the land, to someone like us is

The most wonderful news.

The love, the donations, and willingness to share.

Just knowing that people really do care.

Habitat for Humanity puts an end to strife

And gives people like us a whole new life.

Thank you, Habitat for Humanity.
—Jean Jackson and family

CHAPTER SIX

What Makes It Work?

The Philosophy Behind All Those Hammers and Houses

HOW MUCH money do we need to raise before we begin a Habitat affiliate?" people ask me.

My answer is always the same: "A dollar. If you have less than a dollar, launching a project would be irresponsible." Then I explain that there is another requirement: "You also must have a core group of committed people who are serious about the economics of Jesus and about helping needy people find a simple, decent place to live."

I can say something like that for an undertaking as serious as beginning a Habitat for Humanity affiliate, because of the philosophy that Habitat for Humanity is based upon.

And what is that philosophy?

Actually, I should say there are three philosophies. What we do is based on concepts I call the "theology of the hammer," the "economics of Jesus," and "love in the mortar joints."

The concept of the theology of the hammer is that our Christian faith, actually our entire Judeo-Christian tradition, mandates that we do more than just *talk* about faith and *sing* about love. We must put *faith* and *love* into *action* to make them real. Faith must be incarnate. It must become more than a verbal proclamation or intellectual assent. True faith must be acted out. Love must become real, tangible, and understandable.

How does this thinking manifest itself in Habitat for Humanity? First of all, we believe God has called us to the task of housing the world's poor, and that we are called to work *with* them, be their partners, and not simply do something *for* them. The theology of the hammer also mandates that houses be built and poor families moved in as expressions of love. And the idea requires that continuing love, concern, and guidance be shared to ensure that the families are successful as new homeowners.

It also is about building bridges of understanding with a wide diversity of people in order to put that faith and love into action to accomplish our lofty, seemingly impossible goal of eliminating poverty housing and homelessness. It's acknowledging the differences of opinion—political, philosophical, and theological—among people and being committed to finding common ground with our hammers to help others, using biblical economics.

I call this the economics of Jesus, the second philosophy Habitat for Humanity is built upon—and perhaps the best known. First, we charge no interest and make no profit. This sounds unworkable to our Western minds. But it does work, and it's biblical—based on Exodus 22:25, which says that someone lending money to the poor should not act as a creditor and charge interest.

Interestingly, all three of the world's great monotheistic religions—namely Judaism, Christianity, and Islam—agree in their scriptures that no interest should be charged when lending money to the poor.

But, think about it. We've turned scriptural wisdom upside down. At our lending institutions, the people who need the money most are charged the most. The people who need it least—the rich—are charged the least, the prime rate. Why? Because the world's idea is not to help people, but to make money.

But *our* idea *is* to help people. The economics of Jesus puts no value on profit or interest but does put tremendous emphasis on meeting human need, which is an absolute essential in building homes for and with the poor. Interest is a giant barrier that the poor cannot cross to escape their miserable lifestyle, so they remain mired down in hopelessness.

Another tenet of this philosophy calls for passing out all we have, just like Jesus did with the loaves and fishes. When we do, we can expect a similar result. Small resources have a way of multiplying to the point of meeting the need.

At Koinonia Farm, where the Habitat idea was born, the original Fund for Humanity was always broke. Whatever money came in was immediately spent on building more houses. That has been the model for Habitat. Nothing is held back for investments or endowments. The houses we build *are* the endowment, the most creative one in the world today. The needy families literally "live in the endowment" and their house payments constitute the "dividends" that get used up to build still more houses.

Keeping these ideals—trusting, sharing without seeking profits, making need and not our standard of merit the criterion, passing out everything we have as soon as we have it—we've seen our small gifts multiply into huge dimensions.

With all this talk about the economics of Jesus, why then do we place such emphasis on being ecumenical?

Clarence Jordan of Koinonia Farm introduced me to the God movement—his term for the kingdom of God. The concept was all about being God's partner and partners with one another to do God's work in the world. That means building bridges between people and seeking reconciliation. Habitat for Humanity tries to become all things to all denominations and many different groups of people so that we might encourage them to work together.

Our "theology of the hammer" brings together an incredible array of folks—people who disagree on all sorts of things, both political and theological, but who can all agree on a hammer—the instrument of Jesus, the Carpenter.

I do tell audiences across the country and around the world that Habitat for Humanity does have one doctrinal point, and that is *if you don't have a Habitat bumper sticker on your car, you are living in sin*. I say that in jest, of course, but like most jokes, there *is* some seriousness behind it—since we believe in challenging everybody to join us in our worldwide effort to eliminate poverty housing.

I've said for years in my speeches that every house built by Habitat for Humanity is a house of God. We just let people live in them. I even tell homeowners that they are sleeping on the first pew of God's house.

Everyone laughs, but they understand. This work is about putting God's love into action. Our work does speak for us and for everyone involved.

So, although Habitat for Humanity is overtly Christian, we will be eternally open to and accepting of other religious persuasions, even those who have different motivations. We certainly acknowledge that Christians are not the only folk who know how to express love. What we do is so basic and so right that all religions of the world can agree with our work because all share the intrinsic belief that helping the poor is good.

Habitat for Humanity has certainly put together some very interesting partnerships. Ohio Wesleyan University sent a Habitat work team consisting of Christians, Moslems, Buddhists, and Jews to work with the Columbia, South Carolina Habitat for Humanity.

When we presented a new homeowner family in Buffalo, New York with one of the Bibles we always give at each dedication, the Moslem family gladly accepted it. Then they gave us something in return—a copy of the Koran. Both sides witnessed to what they believed. It was a joyous occasion.

In 1993 and again in 1994, a group of twenty Catholics and Protestants from the Republic of Ireland and Northern Ireland came to the United States to work for twelve weeks on Habitat building sites in Florida, Maryland, and Georgia.

Many non-Christians, especially Jews, are involved in Habitat for Humanity. In fact, participation in our projects by Jewish individuals, congregations, and communities has become quite common over the last few years.

In 1985, fifteen volunteers from the American Jewish Society for Service in New York City spent seven weeks helping build three houses on Habitat Hill in Amarillo, Texas. Since then, this fine organization has worked with Habitat affiliates in several other cities.

The first all-Jewish-built Habitat house was sponsored by Houston's Jewish community in 1993. Then in the summer of 1994, Roanoke, Virginia's Jewish community built the second one, working side by side with Linda Miller and her children, the new owners of the soon-to-be Habitat home. The Roanoke Jewish Community Council, an umbrella organization for donations to a variety of Jewish and Israeli causes, donated almost two-thirds of the money needed to build Linda Miller's house. The rest was donated by individuals. A *Roanoke Times and World News* article reported about the news conference that Rabbi Frank Muller gave at the Habitat work site. He explained that the performance of deeds of loving kindness was one of the three pillars of Judaism. The other duties of study and worship lead the devout to, as he put it, "bring God into the world" through charitable acts. Their motto for the project? "Unless the Lord builds the house, they labor in vain who build it" (Ps. 127:1, NKJV).

Writer Fay Mikowitz, also Jewish, wrote an article in *Woman's Day* magazine about her experience building a Habitat home with us during the 1987 Jimmy Carter Work Project in North Carolina. She was apprehensive that she would be surrounded by Christian missionaries ready to convert her. Instead, she found that her fellow workers who called themselves Christians were, as she expressed it, "shoe-leather Christians" who didn't need to talk about their religion because they lived it out so much in their everyday lives.

(Photo by Julie Lopez)

A volunteer trims roofing shingles on a 30/30,000 house. Habitat builders are young and old, male and female, rich and poor—everyone learning new skills and sharing their talents to help families in need.

Let me tell you a story to illustrate how our brand of love in action is for everyone. One day several years ago, I received a call from a person I'd never heard of. I wouldn't have taken the call normally because I was so busy, but the caller was persistent. So I picked up the phone and heard a woman's voice exulting:

"Millard Fuller, you are a wonderful man!" Immediately I knew I was right to take the call. I thanked her.

"I've just read one of your books, and it's a wonderful book, and you are *wonderful!*" she went on. "But there is one problem."

I knew it was too good to be true. And yet I guessed what was bothering her. She told me she was Jewish. "You don't like the Jesus part of the book, do you?"

There was a stunned silence on the other end. "How did you know?"

"Well," I said, "I've received phone calls similar to this one. You know, I went to Israel recently and discovered that Jesus was a Jew."

"You didn't know that?" she exclaimed.

I laughed. "Yes, I did, " I confessed, "but I was making a point that the Christian religion sprang from a bunch of Jews. We have a lot in common," I pointed out. "The Bible says God has a special love for the Jews, His chosen people."

She warmed up then, telling me that she and her husband owned a small construction company outside New York City and that she'd like to see a Habitat project started there. In good conscience, she said she couldn't serve on a board of directors but would get her Christian friends to form a board, and she'd help raise funds.

"Why don't you and your husband come down to Atlanta and help us at the Jimmy Carter Work Project?" I suggested.

"I told you, I'm Jewish," she said.

"That's not the question. Can you drive a nail? Do you and your husband know how to build a house?"

"Yes," she said, "but there's another problem." She was silent for a moment, then blurted out, "We're Republicans."

"Oh, no!" I exclaimed. "God loves the Jews, but He didn't say anything about *Republicans!* Come to think of it, He didn't mention Democrats either. I still think you should come."

In the days that followed, she called every day with new ideas. When I was invited to speak to a group in New York, she and her whole family met me at the airport dressed in the Habitat tee shirts she'd ordered. Ultimately, she and her husband did come to Atlanta to work with the Jimmy Carter Work Project. Her husband led a construction crew, and they returned home to become very active in forming a local Habitat affiliate. I came to love and respect this lady and her beautiful family. She is not a Christian by her own admission, but she is a special and appreciated partner in the growing, open work of Habitat for Humanity.

We have even had workers who called themselves atheists. They cringed each time God or Jesus was mentioned, but they nevertheless knew a worthy project when they saw one—and continued right on hammering those nails.

This is faith and love in action. This is social action accomplished with private hands from open hearts—based on old, old ideas. Any person of faith recognizes that. Everyone is welcome. Thousands upon thousands of volunteers have caught the vision, which we fondly refer to as "infectious habititis." That "infection" has crossed all boundaries of race, religion, and creed.

To ensure that Habitat reaches out to all races, religions, and creeds, a Diversity Department has been established within Habitat for Humanity International to raise awareness about the mission, projects, and accomplishments of Habitat. It strives to increase the participation and inclusion of minorities in all facets of our work, enhancing understanding and success of our projects in communities of large minority populations, while promoting good race relations through all aspects of our volunteerism and decision-making processes. The thriving partnerships with Delta Sigma Theta and Sigma Gamma Rho are just two examples of the importance of our commitment to diversity.

What does this mean to our "partner families," the people selected for housing?

From the beginning, we have insisted on nondiscriminatory family selection criteria for all Habitat homeowner families, which we believe to be consistent with the universal love of God. No one is excluded from that love. Neither race nor religion determine who will receive a Habitat home. Need is the paramount criterion.

In India, for instance, a Hindu woman once asked the local government authorities if she must become a Christian to be accepted for a Habitat house. The president of the Habitat affiliate in that part of India was called in. "Tell the lady," he said, "that all she needs to know is that God loves her. She was chosen on the basis of her need."

My dream from the outset of Habitat was that our work be a new frontier in Christian missions. This work is a new mission field, an environment where people who normally do not work together can do so to the betterment of their community and those in need. As I've seen this dream come true, I've noticed that so much more than a house is built by Habitat for Humanity.

Maybe one of the unspoken philosophies behind all that we do at Habitat is that of consciousness-raising. In one sense, "unspoken" is not the right word, because quite literally, most of the consciousness-raising in Habitat for Humanity is accomplished via the spoken word.

I speak scores of times each year all across the United States and around the world because I want Habitat for Humanity to be the world's conscience concerning shelter.

I ride in dozens of airplanes every year. I never know who will be sitting beside me, but I do know this: By the time our wheels touch down at the next airport, my seatmate will have heard about Habitat for Humanity. At some point, our conversation will have centered on the worldwide need for housing.

In January 1995, as Linda and I and our Africa Area Director Harry Goodall flew from Addis Ababa, Ethiopia to Cairo, Egypt, my seatmate was a businessman from Athens, Greece. I began to tell him about Habitat for Humanity. He had never heard of it, even though he worked for an American company. He asked many questions and was greatly interested in the work.

He asked why I was going to Cairo. I told him and especially talked about our house-building in one of the big garbage dumps there. He became subdued and somber in his speech. "I spent the first twenty-one years of my life in Cairo," he said. "My father was a businessman there. But when President Nasser came to power, he nationalized businesses.

Dramatic overview of the garbage dump in Cairo, Egypt, where Habitat is building.

Our family lost everything. The whole ordeal was too much for my father. He died the next year." He told me he was a Christian and that he really liked what we were doing in the ministry of Habitat for Humanity. Then he looked at me and asked, "How much does it cost to build one of those houses in the garbage dump of Cairo?"

"Nine hundred dollars," I replied.

Forthwith, he pulled out his wallet and counted out nine one-hundred-dollar bills and gave them to me. "Build one for me," he said. And we did!

Sometimes eyes are opened in dramatic ways creating action without a Habitat affiliate anywhere nearby. A few years ago, I was on a speaking trip in Tupelo, Mississippi before a Habitat affiliate had been formed there. I was invited by a United Methodist pastor, Curtis Petrey, who had a circuit of rural churches near Tupelo. There are some great little towns around Tupelo with names like Algoma, Pontotoc, and Palestine. I spoke in all those places on Saturday and Sunday. On Monday morning while I was having breakfast with Curtis and his wife Nancy, the phone rang. Curtis answered it, and after a brief conversation he returned and sat down with a big smile on his face.

"Millard," he said, "you'll be interested to know what that call was about. A man who heard you in church yesterday called to say that when he walked out of his house this morning, he saw that the house across the street was in pitiful condition. He said he had never noticed it before, and he was so upset that he went to his next-door neighbor— who was also in church yesterday—and asked if he had noticed the condition of the house across the street. The neighbor looked over there and said that he really hadn't seen it either. They both went right over. There's a widow living there on a very limited income; the house is leaking; the walls are falling in; the floor is collapsing. This man was calling to tell me they are both staying out of work today to get started on repairing her house!"

There are as many ways to educate consciences as there are consciences, of course, and our volunteers are constantly coming up with ideas that raise even *our* awareness. Habitat's mission is providing shelter. But because Habitat folks are always concerned about the whole person, a remarkable number of related programs have developed as part of Habitat's ongoing work, and each one offers important reminders of what we are about.

Habitat for Humanity with Disabilities was founded by Joe and Stephanie Thomas in Milledgeville, Georgia. It is a segment of Habitat's ministry that provides technical and financial assistance to affiliates building barrier-free homes for those with disabilities. Habitat for Humanity with Disabilities has set a goal for all Habitat homes to be constructed for barrier-free accessibility.

During our Jimmy Carter Work Project in Milwaukee, barrier-free design consultant Patty Hayes heard we were building one of the houses for a disabled person. She volunteered her expertise; we learned a lot from listening to her, and in the years since we have tried to design more accessibility into the average Habitat home. Some of the building criteria now suggested to affiliates include wider doors and halls and at least

(Habitat for Humanity file photo)

Pleased Habitat homeowner and her children in front of their handicap-accessible home.

one no-step entrance with a sloped walkway where possible. In Americus, for instance, we decided that all Habitat homes would have some additional features including lowered light switches, raised electrical outlets, and wood backing around tubs and toilets for easy installation of grab bars if needed in the future.

Internationally, the need is just as great—if not greater. In Papua New Guinea, Linda and I participated in a dedication of two houses built for people they called "wheelies"—persons who use wheelchairs. One of the "wheelie" families had been living in hospital quarters because most traditional houses there were built on stilts.

Every day we hear of special housing needs. There are requests to build more houses for the elderly, housing for people with Hansen's Disease (leprosy), and chemical-free housing for people suffering from environmental illnesses, to name just a few. Affiliates also are free and willing to tackle their own communities' special needs. For example, Coastal Empire Habitat for Humanity in Savannah, Georgia renovated an old, abandoned house and sold it at no profit and no interest to Hope House of Savannah for a home for unwed, pregnant young women.

Eyeglasses also can raise awareness. In Americus, boxes of used eyeglasses arrive at our office every week. They are sorted, packaged, and shipped in fifty-five-gallon drums to Habitat locations in Africa, South America, and other developing countries where eye problems affect as much as 25 percent of the population. Collecting unwanted eyeglasses and shipping them to Habitat projects overseas, Habitat provides eyeglasses for people in need at a minimal cost, and the returns help build more Habitat houses. In fact, for each fifty-five-gallon drum sold—about eight hundred pairs of glasses—a house can be built. This innovative program is called Vision/Habitat.

We sell many other items that generate both awareness and funds. As I stated in the introduction, profits and royalties from the sale of this book, as well as profits and royalties from all my other books, go to build more houses. Likewise, profits from the sale of tee shirts, hats, bumper stickers, videos, and other products advertised in our catalog, included with each issue of *Habitat World*, go to build more houses. These varied products also promote awareness of the work.

In 1993 we published a cookbook, *Partners in the Kitchen*. Linda served as editor of the highly successful book, which sold more than one hundred thousand copies in the first two years. That produced half a million dollars for house-building. In 1995 we published a second cookbook, this one featuring desserts. We named it *Home Sweet Habitat*. The series will be continued in years to come. This one book series will ultimately produce millions of dollars that will translate into thousands of houses.

Two children's story books about Habitat for Humanity, a Habitat coloring book, and a collection of Thanksgiving and Christmas stories entitled *Home for the Holidays*, also were published in 1995. We also are exploring importing items made by Habitat homeowners in developing countries to sell in the United States. That will generate income both for the homeowners and for building more houses—another win/win deal!

The Habitat for Homeless Humanity program grew out of a deep concern for people who have no shelter at all. Habitat's main goal is to help the "invisible" homeless, those living in substandard housing. But how can we ignore the people on the streets? This program offers opportunities and suggestions on ways affiliates can aid the homeless and provide transitional housing for homeless individuals.

Some Habitat affiliates already were building and renovating houses for homeless people. In New York City, when the Habitat affiliate renovated a building for nineteen low-income families, one of the apartments was allotted to a man who had been living in a box behind the building. In Atlanta, one of the twenty houses built during the Jimmy Carter Work Project in 1988 was for a man and three children who moved into their new home from a shelter. He had a job but couldn't afford housing because his income was so low. An affiliate in North Carolina built a house with a family living in an abandoned bus. So did an affiliate in west Georgia. A new Habitat affiliate in Hawaii selected a homeless family previously living in a fire station. These homeless people applied for homeownership and met the requirements of being able to make the small mortgage payments as well as the sweat equity requirement.

To help such people, local Habitat affiliates work with other groups to provide shelter for homeless people. The mayor of Charleston, South Carolina created a task force to help his city's homeless. All sorts of groups, from the Salvation Army to the Veterans Administration to Habitat for Humanity, responded to the call for help. Habitat's part was to organize the construction of 264-square-foot, heated cottages for men coming out of a local shelter. Habitat for Homeless Humanity encourages affiliates to look for creative ways to help the homeless in their area, especially the homeless who ultimately might be capable of Habitat homeownership if given a helping hand.

These and other programs continue to keep us on our toes, our own consciousness raised in the process. How can people meet needs unless they can see those needs? Habitat strives to open eyes as well as hearts.

The way we go about bringing all the materials, money, and land together for each housing project is also part of the idea that drives Habitat for Humanity.

In Habitat, we are always trying to link up people and resources to get the job done. It's a continuing process, and I learned a long time ago that you get more money by asking than not asking. And when you ask, things happen.

Another deeply held philosophy of Habitat is what I call "the man with the land."

That, of course, requires a story to explain it. One night several years ago, Linda and I attended a Habitat meeting in north Georgia. After chatting awhile with the leaders of the newly formed group, we found out they were making good progress. They'd incorporated, committees had been formed, and some money had been raised. There was only one problem: They didn't have any land. They had searched and searched but could not find any suitable building sites. So when I spoke that night, I addressed the land problem.

"You don't have any land, I understand," I said. "I find that a bit strange. When we drove into town a while ago, I saw land everywhere. It was on the right side of the road and the left. Even the road was built on *land.* Most of you here this evening are strangers to me. I don't know you personally. I don't know about your finances, abilities, or possessions. But I do know that you've got land. I don't know who's got what, but I know you've got it—and God knows too. It all belongs to Him anyway.

"So," I ventured, "what I want tonight is for the person who has some of God's property that could be used by your new Habitat affiliate to come forward and let us know who you are. We'll solve this land problem quickly."

When I finished speaking a distinguished, silver-haired gentleman came forward and said, "*I'm the man with the land.* While you were talking about it, my wife almost poked my ribs out! I'll have my lawyer make the deed out next week."

A few weeks later, I was visiting a new Habitat affiliate in south Georgia. The project leaders said essentially the same thing: Everything seemed to be falling into place—except for the land. So, of course, I again asked for the *man with the land* to come forward. And again, "the man" came right up after I finished speaking.

Later, while on a speaking tour in California, I was with a local Habitat affiliate that had just completed its first three houses. The group wanted to build more, but guess what? No land. So you know what I did. When I spoke, I told the other two "man with the land" stories. When I ended my speech, a man came forward who said he had a tract of land he wanted to donate—large enough to build seventeen houses.

Such responses kept coming, one right after another. Then one day on a speaking tour in the Northwest, I learned the project leaders in Bend, Oregon were in the same predicament: Everything was in place but the land. So when I spoke, I once more told my "man with the land" stories. But this time, I asked, "Isn't it about time for a *woman* with the land to come forward?" I told the crowd I knew for a fact that men do not own *all* the land.

At the end of the meeting, no one came forward. Not a woman. Not a man. No one. It was a little discouraging, especially since the crowd was a large one—several hundred people—and "land" was written all over many of the faces. That night, though, as I enjoyed some late-night refreshments with the couple hosting me, they said that perhaps *they* were the people with the land since they had a large lot they could give.

Then the next morning, during coffee hour at the Habitat office, a woman walked in and handed me a real estate sales contract. She announced that *she was the woman with the land* and that the two lots were now Habitat's. After that announcement, she smiled, patted me on the back, and left.

That's the way it happens—the way our houses get built. Be it land or services or building materials or money or whatever, connections are made that result in houses being built. Everyone has different reasons for why he or she gives. What we know is that there is always a good reason for giving—a personal reason, as well as the fact that a house is waiting to be built and lives will be changed because of it. We just have to ask.

One of my biggest frustrations is people who claim to be Christians and to love their neighbors but spend lavishly on themselves, then throw crumbs over the fence to those in need.

Unfortunately there's a trend in this country to build bigger and bigger houses. Everybody wants bigger houses. One of the real ironies of modern life is that the typical American wage-earner is making his or her maximum income just as the children are leaving home. So precisely when the average American family needs less house, they typically build or buy a bigger one—not because they need the bigger house but because they can afford it. The policies of our government actually encourage building houses bigger than we need because if we sell our small house, make a profit, and don't invest it in a bigger house, we have to pay taxes on the profit. So the government is actually encouraging people to build bigger and bigger houses. Within the context of this societal mentality, everybody feels it's natural to be constantly acquiring or building bigger houses.

The poor are not immune to this mentality. They too want to get bigger houses. In low-income neighborhoods, the tension can be the same as in middle-class or rich neighborhoods. In the Watts neighborhood of south Los Angeles, for example, the Jimmy Carter Work Project scheduled for June 1995 came to the brink of cancellation because there was so much clamor in the neighborhood to build bigger houses. It was not because the people *needed* bigger houses, but because the people who already lived there felt that if Habitat built modest homes—simple, decent houses, which is what we do—their real estate values would go down. They were demanding that Habitat build houses as big as the biggest homes in the neighborhood or even bigger. Why? So the neighborhood would become upwardly mobile instead of "downwardly."

In their opinion, when smaller houses are built the neighborhood becomes characterized as a low-income neighborhood. They wanted to be characterized as a

Checking the window frame installation on one of the thirty new Habitat houses completed in Americus in June 1994.

(Photo by Tally Lancaster)

middle-class or upper-class neighborhood in order for their real estate investments to remain high and go even higher. That's why the people in the neighborhood were clamoring for Habitat to build eighteen-hundred-square-foot houses which we could not build for less than $80,000 to $100,000 each. The problem was eventually resolved, with Habitat building modest houses.

A recent *Chicago Tribune* article told of this very conflict in Elgin, Illinois with a bit of a twist. Although the Habitat house was being built in an area troubled with gangs, litter, graffiti, and small, aging houses including flats designed for factory workers decades ago, the Habitat lot was just down the street from an area of hundred-year-old Victorian homes that could qualify the neighborhood as a national historical site, something the city wanted to happen. They believed Habitat's simple house (or "ugly" house, as a member of the area's Heritage Commission called it) might hinder the chances. The commission member pointed more to its lack of style, a house "devoid of architectural features," as the reason for the resistance rather than the idea of having poor people living near the area with such potential of being "gentrified."

In this instance, the city reimbursed Habitat for Humanity for the costs already incurred on the lot—around fifty thousand dollars—leaving the already-laid foundation just sitting there while the affiliate took the money and started over elsewhere.

In Atlanta, the Habitat affiliate planned to build four houses on land donated by a town in the metro area. Neighbors in nearby Willow Springs Country Club subdivision objected. One man in that subdivision told the *Atlanta Journal and Constitution*, "If they agree to build something that meets our standards of $200,000 houses, we have no problem. Habitat can build a $200,000 house. Why not?" Eventually, the land was given back to the town and Atlanta Habitat for Humanity built in another, friendlier neighborhood.

So there is increasing pressure from many neighborhoods for Habitat to build bigger and bigger houses, while failing to appreciate our "simple, decent place to live" concept. It has nothing to do with the needs of the families. It's economic protection, or a "keeping up with the Joneses" mentality. It is hard to fight, but it's an attitude that most Americans have been taught.

This mentality is not restricted to the United States. In March 1995, a groundbreaking for some new Habitat houses was held in Vac, Hungary, a small town on the Danube River twenty miles north of Budapest. Habitat volunteer Stephen Kazella wrote about the reception:

> "We arrived to the dismay of the neighbors, who had pulled out the survey stakes the previous day. As our program got underway, the neighbors tried to obstruct the ceremony by playing loud Christian rock music. Kalman Lorenz, the Habitat for Humanity national director for Hungary, seizing the moment, invited them to join in the digging, with a big smile. Hands were joined and raised and a prayer said for the completion of the houses. We all grabbed a shovel and began to dig the foundations. The lot was transformed, literally, in a few hours."

Even in the poorest developing nations, there are numerous wealthy people, and many see their wealth and often extravagant lifestyles as an absolute right with no responsibilities toward those who are less fortunate. Few of them are known for their generosity toward their poor countrymen. They build walls around themselves to keep the poor away. The idea of helping their fellow citizens in need seems ridiculous.

I recall once traveling on a plane in Zaire. I was seated next to a wealthy Zairian businessman. He knew who I was, and I knew of him. He started talking to me about the housing program in Mbandaka and suddenly blurted out, "Monsieur Fuller, I would like you to build me a house. I already have four houses, and I would like you to build me another."

"Citoyen," I addressed him, using the Zairian courtesy title, "concerned people in the United States, Canada, and Europe have given money for building houses for the poor. Since you are quite wealthy, I'd like to ask *you* to donate to the project, to help your own poor countrymen have better housing."

He was amazed. He fixed me with a long stare and retorted, "I'm not interested in giving money away! I want to make more!"

In the Western world, there is a tradition of helping the poor. The basis of this is, of course, the Bible. Unfortunately, an increasing number of affluent people everywhere are thinking like this Zairian businessman, and worse—some claiming God's blessings as the reason for their lack of feeling for the poor. They feel no obligation to share.

While on a visit to a Habitat affiliate in Nebraska, my host drove me past the new $6.5 million home of a local business tycoon. It was enormous, surrounded by a high fence. I was told the owner had installed buzzers in the house so family members could find each other. No one seemed to think this strange; if he could build such a house for himself and his loved ones, he *should* build it.

A national executive of a wealthy Protestant denomination whose support I had requested for Habitat once told me simply that with all of the other needs in the world, "Housing is just not a priority with our mission board." This attitude struck me as a curious double standard, because I had visited the man's home. His house was very large and expensive. In *his* life, housing obviously had a *very* high priority!

In this country, we take our housing for granted. But the best cure for that is to see what Habitat volunteers see. It's hard to ever be callous about shelter, once you see the transformation a simple, decent place has made in the lives of those who move from shacks and the streets into a good house.

In 1949, the United States Congress established a national policy stating that everyone should have a decent place to live. We have not lived up to that ideal. Millions of Americans live in miserable conditions. Hundreds of thousands have no place at all to live. Habitat for Humanity is a voice or conscience for the noble and *achievable* goal of providing a simple, decent place to live . . . for everyone.

"What changes things," said Jack Kemp, commenting on Habitat's impact, "is giving people a stake in the system." If we do, they'll defend it. "What it takes," he says, "is mayors, bank presidents, property owners, and anyone else willing to get involved to work together. . . . It really takes that local commitment, the willingness of people to advance credit, to provide property, to come together to build a house."

I believe that's true. One of the reasons Habitat stays away from government funding for house-building is that our philosophy is a grass-roots one—a vibrant, viable, dynamic grass-roots movement of people motivated by faith and love. We want no strings-attached money that might dampen our vision or beliefs, or "easy" money that might squelch the spirit of our incredible network of donors and volunteers. Blessings involved with giving and receiving are powerful indeed, and even more powerful in changing lives when offered from the individual heart.

Yet I honestly don't think we can live up to the high ideal passed in 1949 without the involvement of the government. There are several countries in the world today that have no poverty housing. In every one of those countries, there is extensive government involvement in housing. So there must be some government involvement in any plan to eliminate poverty housing, but it should be wise involvement. What we're proposing, and what some politicians are now embracing is the idea that government set the stage; then with private resources, Habitat can build on that stage.

And what does "setting the stage" mean? It means providing land, streets, sidewalks, donating old buildings to be renovated, perhaps providing some funds for administrative expenses, etc. Then individuals, churches, corporations, and other organizations with private resources can begin to build on that stage. This method maximizes the effectiveness of both the government and the private sector.

Sometimes government can actually *create* barriers to Habitat building. Perhaps they don't want the poor to live in certain areas, so they can make it hard to get land, sewer hook-ups, electricity, and water. Or maybe they charge exorbitant fees for the privilege of building for the poor. But if government paves the way, eliminates these sorts of barriers, and aggressively helps organizations such as Habitat, then a workable partnership is formed, and things will change for the better. Quickly!

Of course, there is also the other extreme, and that doesn't work either: the idea that government should do it all.

"Here's something we've built for you," the government says. "Move in and behave." Then people move in and tear it up. Why?

Human beings are the most sensitive creatures on earth. If I deal with you in such a way that you are led to believe, based on abundant evidence, that I have a very low opinion of you, you will respond accordingly. My attitude says to you, "Oh, you poor ignorant person! I have a societal responsibility to take care of you, so I've prepared some chicken-house-like dwellings for you to live in; they are all alike, because *you* are all alike. You can't own them because you're not capable of ownership. You're obviously too stupid."

It isn't surprising that people who are treated this way feel no responsibility for the property involved, and no hope of breaking free from the circumstances that brought them to this point in their lives.

Habitat for Humanity, on the other hand, says to this same person, "I consider you to be a very intelligent person. Everybody needs help sometimes. At this particular point in your life, you need a house. As a fellow human being, I want to work not for you, but *with* you. So let's work together to build a house. You're going to help build it and when it's finished, it's going to be yours. You're going to get a deed to it, and you'll make monthly payments. You're going to be paying for your own house. The money you pay will go to help others have houses too. In the meantime, you can select your paint colors and be involved in designing the house."

After that sort of treatment by Habitat, how would this person feel?

"That's *my* house," the person will say. "I helped build it. I spent hundreds of hours building it. I put this wall in right here. I know exactly where the electrical lines are; they're right here. This is *my house,* all right. I not only have a deed to it, but I feel within myself that *it is my house.*"

Hope and pride of ownership change everything. Give a person some dignity, hope, and gratitude—then stand back and see the positive results.

We must look at the housing problem this way. Instead of attempting to ignore the poor, it is only common sense and in the enlightened self-interest for the community to help its own. But that help must be administered in a way that is uplifting, empowering, and strengthening—not demeaning. There's a big difference.

Think about it this way: Imagine you have an injured leg. There are two ways to deal with your injury—either hold your leg up with a crutch and do without its use for the rest of your life, or strengthen the leg and put it back into full use, eventually insisting that it carry its part of the load. Failure to strengthen the leg will cause it to become dependent and helpless—atrophied from nonuse.

Much of the error in our government's welfare programs comes from this failure to strengthen, to nurture those in need into productive self-sufficiency. The government says, "You are poor. We'll just carry you for the rest of your lives. Here's where to pick up the check." No time or resources are given to guiding these people back to carrying their own weight. How can the rest of their community feel healthy, carrying more than their fair share of the load? Habitat's enlightened philosophy is to *help people help themselves.*

That's why we expect our homeowners to pay their mortgages and pull their own weight. Habitat does not offer charity. Each of the mortgage payments paid by Habitat homeowners is essential to the building of the next house. We treat the homeowners as partners and as responsible adults. We choose them as wisely as we can, for their need and for their willingness to be faithful to their commitment of sweat equity and mortgage payments. In essence, the idea is the best of the traditions of our country. Tens of millions of Americans are descendants of immigrants. The American way always has been to help a newly arrived person become a strong, fully integrated member of the community, for the sake of the person and the future of the country. We want to help bring those who have been left behind back into the fullness of fellowship with their neighbors.

So, we do not convey the message that the new homeowners are "wards" of Habitat for Humanity. No—we say, "This is a partnership—a two-way partnership. We're going to treat you like partners, not like children expected to be permanently dependent on us. As homeowners, you now have a responsibility to us, to others, and to yourselves."

In some countries, this is a hard idea to convey. I mentioned earlier the story of the Zairians who needed peer pressure to remain faithful to their commitment to their community. A few families decided that they really didn't have to make their Habitat monthly payments because they believed Habitat for Humanity, being a Christian organization, probably wouldn't evict them. When we realized this, we stopped all construction work. Soon Habitat leaders were naming names on local radio of the selfish few who were preventing the construction of additional homes, since their payments were integral to the process of buying materials for the next houses in the project. In a few days, the families were once again paying their payments.

These ideas are part of our philosophy of "love in the mortar joints." Some of it is tough love! The whole idea is to do more than just build a bunch of houses. We want to build people too. We want to engage in real partnership that causes growth in individuals and families.

Every Habitat affiliate's Family Selection Committee receives applications from needy families, interviews them, and chooses which families will receive Habitat houses. This committee, or a separate one, functions as a nurturing group to the homeowner—to make sure they participate fully in the building or renovating of their houses and that they fully understand what Habitat for Humanity is all about.

After the houses are finished and the families move in, the nurturers stay with them, help- ing in every way possible to

(Habitat for Humanity file photo)

Millard Fuller concentrates on the task at hand.

ensure their success as new homeowners. The nurturer's relationship always is that of partner and never a condescending one of master, boss, or dictator. Love is the central ingredient that holds the relationship together.

This dual building of houses and people is at the very core of Habitat for Humanity. It is essential to the ongoing and growing success of this move- ment of hammering out not just nails, but also faith and love. In essence, what we are doing is putting "love in the mortar joints."

How do the new Habitat homeowners fare in the United States?

According to a 1993 U.S. Affiliate Census, 89 percent of Habitat homeowners make their payments on time. With 71 percent of affiliates responding, the report also revealed a less than 1 percent foreclosure rate. What makes these figures even more impressive is that they signify that Habitat homeowners are facing and overcoming obstacles, and they affirm that affiliates are effectively resolving problems.

But what, you may ask, keeps the families from taking the house, then reselling it for a profit? That's a question posed to me quite often. This question is usually asked by a solid, middle-class American who thinks like a solid, middle-class person. If you had an investment that you paid thirty thousand dollars for and knew you could sell it for sixty thousand dollars, you'd be tempted to sell it and make a thirty-thousand-dollar profit, wouldn't you? In our experience, low-income families don't think like that. In the two decades of Habitat for Humanity, and even going all the way back to Koinonia Partnership Housing twenty-five years ago, we have had no history of people selling their houses. Why? Because it's so hard for these families to get the houses in the first place. It's like an impossible dream come true. The fact that they can make a profit is not even an issue because they realize that if they sell it they won't have a house any more. And they wouldn't be able to make payments the way the world would demand on a new one, since the bank or someone else attempting to make a big profit would now be the lender.

Let's say a person who fits the Habitat homeowner profile buys a Habitat house for thirty thousand dollars which is really worth sixty thousand dollars. Say they sell it for sixty thousand dollars, thus realizing a thirty-thousand-dollar profit. But they no longer have a house; where will they live? If they cannot buy another Habitat house, it's going to take the whole thirty-thousand-dollar profit—and then some—to purchase yet another house. The interest charged on the balance due would be two or three times the monthly payments they were making on the Habitat house. So what would be the point?

Still, one of the ways to alleviate this worry is to attach a special second mortgage to the house. The house worth sixty thousand dollars is still sold to the family for thirty thousand dollars. The mortgage they sign is a thirty-thousand-dollar no-interest mortgage which they will pay over twenty years. The second mortgage is for the other thirty thousand dollars, which the family will pay for by living in the house. They won't make any monetary payments on the second mortgage, but in the first year 1/20th of it will be forgiven, the second year another 1/20th will be forgiven, and so on for the next twenty years.

The first mortgage will be satisfied with money, while the second mortgage will be paid by living in the house. That way, both mortgages will be wiped out at the end of twenty years, and the homeowners can own their home free and clear.

But in the unlikely event that a homeowner may live there one year, then decide to bail out and sell the house for the aforementioned sixty thousand dollars, Habitat will receive 19/20ths of the profit and the homeowner will receive just 1/20th of the profit. That way, if there is a legitimate reason that the homeowner must sell, the family would still gain some profit to start over elsewhere, yet the affiliate would once again own the property to sell to another homeowner.

Add that to the first buy-back option clause that many affiliates put into their agreement with the new homeowners, and our middle-class worries are alleviated. Again, it's a win/win situation for all concerned. The vast majority of homeowner families feel a deep sense of attachment to their new home—this miracle of housing that is theirs for a lifetime.

Over and above all our philosophies, the one thing that drives the idea of Habitat for Humanity for everyone is that this crazy idea makes sense. This basic truth continues to keep the fires burning at home and abroad, regardless of race or creed.

Radical common sense!

Once when I was speaking at the University of Akron, I was introduced as Millard Fuller, "the man who heads an organization that practices radical common sense." That's what the philosophy of Habitat truly is—radical common sense.

What do I mean by that?

It's radical in several ways. First, there is the notion that we can eliminate substandard housing and homelessness—that's a radical, seemingly impossible dream. Second, it's radical to attack something so big, so bold, to go at cross-currents with the economic stream of society. By not charging interest and selling houses at no profit, we are out of sync with the ways of the world. But, as stated earlier, the only way to enable the poor to no longer be poor is to take the burden of interest off their backs. In the Western world, which is supposedly so heavily influenced by the Judeo-Christian tradition, we have taken the idea and turned it upside down. In our society the richest members receive the prime (lowest) lending rate and the poorest, who need it most, instead are charged the highest rate.

In Habitat for Humanity, we're taking the radical path—trying to do business with ancient wisdom. When we first began doing it, I actually heard people say, "You're going to build houses at no interest, no profit? That sounds un-American, like some Communist scheme."

I'd answer, "But it's in the Bible."

The usual response? "Well, you're not going to take the Bible *that* seriously, are you? It's not for the practical, work-a-day world. The Bible is all right for church and Sunday school, but not for the middle of the week."

I read an article recently about Joe Slovo, who at the time was head of housing for South Africa's government. A Communist, he was promoting market economy ideas.

"But you're a Communist!" his detractors said. "Well," he responded, "consider me a Communist like most Christians are Christians. It's OK for the sweet by-and-by, but has nothing to do with the reality of the here and now."

Ouch! But it's true, isn't it? Habitat, then, is radical because of our goals and methodology, but we're also radical because we challenge people to put their religion into practice, and because we encourage conservatives and liberals, blacks and whites, rich and poor, Catholics and Protestants and other divergent individuals and groups to work together.

Yet the idea is so full of common sense. Why? Because everybody who gets sleepy at night should have a simple, decent place to sleep—on terms they can afford to pay. Since we all get sleepy, we know this is true. No one can disagree with such a logical statement. No one can disagree that the place we lay our heads should be a clean and decent one, and that it can make all the difference in our lives.

I received a letter recently that clearly illustrates how the common sense of Habitat's mission still wins out over even the most serious reservations:

A woman from Florida wrote, "I am outraged at your blatant Christianity. My parents freed me from the myth of religion. So I'm disgusted that you talk in religious slogans and scriptures. But I just love what you do. I think it's great you build houses for families, and I like the way you do it with no profit, no interest, sweat equity, and getting everybody to work together. So enclosed is my latest contribution of $100. . . . "

These are the concepts, then, behind our crazy idea that works. It works because the philosophies are as sound as they are radical, and deeply sensible in the grand scheme of things.

When taken seriously, when taken straight to heart, these ideas must inspire us to begin thinking about and ultimately embracing one central idea for ourselves and for our community, wherever we live.

We must all begin to say that it is unacceptable—politically, socially, and religiously—for people to live in subhuman conditions.

This must stop.

CHAPTER SEVEN

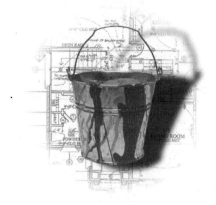

Who Are These Volunteers and Why Are They Doing What They Do?

Habitat's Volunteer Explosion

JIMMY CARTER OFTEN comments about the joy he and Rosalynn have experienced, working as volunteers with Habitat for Humanity. In his keynote address at one of our big celebrations, he told the crowd, "Rosalynn and I are often asked, 'Why do you work with Habitat? What do you get out of it?' I was president of the United States for four years, but I get a lot more recognition for building houses in partnership with poor people in need than I ever got for the Camp David Accord or SALT I. I can walk down the aisles of airplanes and invariably the number one thing that anybody who stops me ever says is, 'Tell me about Habitat. . . .' Habitat is not a sacrifice that we make for others. It is a blessing for those of us who volunteer to help others. It gives me a life of excitement and pleasure, and adventure and unpredictability, to put it mildly. . . . It is the most rewarding and joyful activity we are engaged in."

A hard day's work for something worthwhile is what some volunteers call a day with Habitat. George Peagler, Jr., an Americus attorney and chairman of the Sumter County Initiative, worked as a volunteer when his church sponsored a blitz house. In an article in *Men's Journal,*

131

he said he loves organizing work but is always itching to get out to the construction site. "I do a lot of litigation of cases that sometimes takes three to four years to complete," he explained. "The satisfaction of completing a project in an afternoon—even if it's just putting up a wall—helps a lot."

Sometimes I say that Habitat for Humanity offers people a way to put their faith into action. In an interview, Rosalynn Carter expressed another essential reason why people volunteer for Habitat work. "We can get so bogged down with just going to work," she said, "that it's important to add this sort of helping or caring element to our lives."

And Habitat volunteers do just that . . . by the thousands. They come in all shapes, sizes, races, and religious persuasions. Volunteers can be any age. Of course, the available tasks are sometimes limited when volunteers are very young or quite elderly. But there are ways to help for anyone, any age, who wants to help.

A group of neighborhood children cut grass, washed windows, and raked yards to collect money for a playground near dozens of Habitat homes in the Optimist Park section of Charlotte, North Carolina.

On his fourth birthday, Jonathan Pittman of Tupelo, Mississippi emptied his piggy bank of its $2.92 and told his mother he wanted to give it to Habitat for Humanity. Jonathan had heard about building houses for the poor from his parents and at Sunday school.

Seven-year-old Amelia Rhodenwalt had been saving her allowance to buy a doll. On her birthday, her Grandma Mary gave her the doll she had wanted. She wondered what she should do with the money she had saved. Then she remembered the people who don't have houses, so she put her savings in the family Habitat money box. Her dad took the money to the next meeting of their local affiliate, Habitat for Humanity of the Coachella Valley in southern California. It was decided that the money should be used to buy a doorbell for a Habitat house which was nearing completion in Palm Desert. Amelia was invited to go with a small delegation to purchase the doorbell. They tested practically every doorbell on display in the store before finding the perfect one. A few days later, Amelia went to the house and helped Randy, the electrician, wire up the doorbell. She reported that it made her feel so good to help finish the new house for the Habitat family.

A sixth-grade class at Mesarobles School in Hacienda Heights, California sent a check to Habitat headquarters, along with this letter written by a class member:

> Our class raised $178 by having a bake sale and chipping in part of our allowances. My class had a controversial debate on what we would like to spend the money for. And we came to a conclusion: we decided to buy seven blocks, a toilet, a door, and a wall.

A remarkable teenager, Amanda Massey, fifteen, of Athens, Alabama, was elected in early 1995 to the board of directors of Athens-Limestone County Habitat for Humanity, becoming the youngest Habitat affiliate board member in the country. This is yet another way to serve as a volunteer for Habitat for Humanity.[1]

Amanda Massey, fifteen, serves on the board of directors of the Athens-Limestone County Habitat for Humanity, making her the youngest affiliate board member in the nation. *

(Habitat for Humanity file photo)

*Note—In many states, laws provide that an individual must be at least eighteen, nineteen, or twenty-one years of age to serve on the board of a nonprofit corporation. Those planning to elect young board members should check their state's laws regarding this matter.

Some volunteers keep coming back to help. One such volunteer is Bill Eaton of Goshen, Indiana. The energetic seventy-year-old retired cabinet maker had put in over one thousand hours of volunteer work on Habitat houses in his local area each year since 1992! And as of the end of 1994, he was still going strong. "Framing, dry wall, painting, setting cabinets, doors, trim—I do about all of it," Bill says. He also works closely with the new homeowner families, teaching them valuable construction skills. During his first three years of volunteer work, he helped build fourteen houses. Bill explained that people helped him when he was growing up and then raising his family. "So," he said, "I thought I could give something back."

Stan George and his wife Helen have been volunteering to help Habitat for Humanity for several years in a most unusual way. These octogenarians from Duarte, California created "George Partners" to match contributions to Habitat for Humanity, the American Bible Society, and Heifer Project. Through tireless efforts, they have raised literally a few million dollars for these three organizations, with hundreds of thousands of dollars designated for the work of Habitat in their local area and overseas. Until recently, Stan rode his motorcycle all over the country making speeches and raising money for Habitat and the other causes he believes in. Stan is a retired Presbyterian minister who believes faith should be acted out and that God put him on this earth to help folks in need. He boldly proclaims the love of Christ in everything he does. Stan and Helen are inspirations to all who know them.

One of Habitat's most dynamic and committed volunteers is Frank Basler of Tryon, North Carolina. He helped start the local affiliate, Thermal Belt Habitat for Humanity, and has consistently pushed and nudged his fellow board members to build more houses locally and overseas. Frank also launched a resale store that receives and sells donated furniture and other household items with the proceeds being used to build Habitat houses. This innovative store has generated tens of thousands of dollars for the ongoing work in that area of western North Carolina. Finally, Frank serves as coordinator of our national board of advisors, a special group of over two hundred volunteers who advise me as president of Habitat for Humanity, and assist as occasion demands in fund-raising and other needs of the overall ministry.

In March 1995 I was on a speaking assignment in Winter Park, Florida. I learned that one of the most faithful volunteers with the local Habitat affiliate was a ninety-two-year-old man. He came out one day a week to help with the construction work. When others would take a break to have some refreshments, he would go to his car for a nap. Otherwise, he worked a full day just like everyone else.

A few years ago on another speaking trip in Arizona, I met an eighty-year-old man who was construction foreman for the local affiliate. "I retired some years back," he told me, "and I played golf for the first ten years. Finally, I got bored. Then I started volunteering with Habitat. I've now been doing that for ten years—and those years have been the best of my life!"

As these examples illustrate, anyone can volunteer. Anyone can help build a house, raise money, prepare meals for the workers, or help in some other way. My advice is to take the first step and see what happens—and what happens is usually contagious. For instance, in October 1994, Kathleen Bowman, the new president of Randolph-Macon Woman's College in Lynchburg, Virginia, by-passed more traditional inauguration ceremonies to encourage a community-based theme that included the building of a Habitat house by Bowman and hundreds of college students, faculty, and alumni. The highlight of the inaugural event? The dedication of the house that the new president helped build! [2]

Diane Nunnelee, a former director of volunteer services at Habitat headquarters, once defined the volunteer role this way:

> "In the way the world works, who can imagine entrusting the construction of homes, the administration of projects, the recruitment of volunteers, the management of contributions . . . to people who ask little or nothing in material reward? But then Habitat is not about doing things the way the world does. Perhaps that is why people volunteer. It affirms gifts and skills offered in love. It is a witness to the truth of the gospel promise that 'as you give, so you shall receive.' Each new volunteer brings a new vitality, a new spirit of willingness, new questions, and new answers. They keep us focused on who we are as they demand of Habitat a consistency in being who we say we are."

How many volunteers are we talking about? They number into the hundreds of thousands and the numbers keep growing. Dramatically. They give millions of hours of service to stuff envelopes, make speeches, attend board meetings, order building supplies, lay foundations, put up walls, nail on shingles, raise money, and much more.

Why are all these people doing so much?

The reasons are as varied as the people. Bill Eaton said he volunteered to "give back." He also said he simply enjoyed working with his hands. Some volunteers thoroughly enjoy organizational work, serving on a board of directors or a committee. I think most would say that they want to give expression to their religious faith and to the love they feel in their hearts. They want to make a difference in their local communities and impact the world. Many volunteer because they want to be a part of the excitement of the mushrooming Habitat for Humanity movement. They want to contribute to something much bigger than themselves. They want to meet and work with Habitat homeowners and interact with interesting people whom they would otherwise never encounter.

We all live in different kinds of circles. Habitat cuts across all those circles to bring people together who would normally never work together. So it's easy to see how people get "hooked" by working in partnership with those in need.

The following story is a good example of the hundreds of true-life situations.

In South Carolina, Habitat volunteer Ed Walpole looked out a window of his home and saw a tornado coming at him in full force. He ran to the basement and threw himself on the floor. He could hear the glass shattering and wind whipping through the upstairs. After a few minutes it was all over. The house was devastated. Ed got up, thankful to be alive, now worrying about his wife Betty who had been driving home when the tornado hit.

When news flashed on television about the tornado damage in Charleston, Habitat homeowner Pedro Suchil immediately thought about his friends, Betty and Ed Walpole. The Walpoles were Pedro's Habitat sponsors. He called to make sure they had not been hurt and then drove out to see for himself. By that time, Betty had arrived home safe, and Pedro insisted that they come and stay in his Habitat house for safety—at least for the night.

It frequently happens that social and psychological barriers are torn down during a Habitat build. As houses go up, loving friendships develop—another wonderful by-product of Habitat volunteerism.

Each new year seems to see the creation of new programs and new excitement by our volunteers. Mix all sorts of people with all sorts of talents and we come up with some grand, fun, useful ideas. One of those ideas that has literally exploded across the country is directly related to the kind of volunteers inspired by the new president of Randolph-Macon Woman's College.

It is our Campus Chapters program, and the volunteers are college and university students, faculty and administration personnel, and high-school students too. The very idea for Campus Chapters came from volunteer Gary Cook, who conceived of the program in 1987 while serving as director of denominational and community relations and assistant to the president at Baylor University in Waco, Texas. Today, Dr. Cook is president of Dallas Baptist University. (Incidentally, the complete and very exciting story of the creation of the Campus Chapters Initiative is told in *The Excitement is Building*, published by Word in 1990.)

Students are a dynamic new movement within Habitat for Humanity, and the importance of Campus Chapters can't be overstated. In fact, I think our Campus Chapters program is the most important program within Habitat, because the youth who become involved today are the adults who will lead the work tomorrow. Campus Chapters director Sonja Lewis puts it this way:

> "Students are a lifeline to Habitat. Many college students who are involved in the Campus Chapters program go on to found, or become board chairpersons of, or in some way get involved with, affiliates. If a survey were taken, I'm certain that we'd find at least 50 percent of those alumni once involved in a Campus Chapter are still involved at their local level today."

With 350 campus chapters and more than nine hundred associate groups on U.S. campuses and seven chapters in other countries, the eight-year-old program already is playing a big role in spreading the work and philosophy of Habitat for Humanity.

Spring break, that collegiate icon of beach antics and loafing in the sun, has become a Habitat-house-building time as all over the country, college groups are rolling up their sleeping bags and going out to meet the "invisible" poor and their needs. More than 4,300 college students took part in the Collegiate Challenge Spring Break of 1994 and over five thousand signed on in 1995.

As one leader from the University of New Hampshire Campus Chapter put it, "Expectations were to build a house and work with a

(Photo by Julie Lopez)

Young people learn quickly about Habitat's principle of sweat equity, as did Claudia Muro, student at Villanova University, during this 1993 Collegiate Challenge scene at Clarksdale, Mississippi.

family. Much, much more happened because we all learned sociology, geography, anthropology, religion, spirituality, and construction."

In fact, campus chapters are getting so good at building that they often build houses on their own. For example, the house at 4961 Stiles Street in Philadelphia was gutted and rebuilt completely by members of Habitat's Drexel University Campus Chapter. "When they first saw what they had to do," laughed the local affiliate's director Catherine Minnis, "they nearly ran away." The row house was a mess, a mere shell. But as the project got off the ground, more and more students came on board. Soon, the project was humming right along.

As an added bonus to the Philadelphia project, the directors were able to seek grants otherwise not available for Habitat projects. "Some funders are more interested in education projects than bricks and mortar. They like to hear about a project where architectural engineers are getting training," said Habitat for Humanity West Philadelphia's Development Director Sheldon Rich.

From Colorado State to Michigan State, from the University of North Carolina to Cornell, college students are taking the initiative, planning, funding, and building houses from start to finish. The Campus Chapter at Salisbury State University, Salisbury, Maryland sponsored two houses with the local Habitat affiliate. Linda and I were privileged to be present to dedicate the first house in early May 1995. That evening eleven hundred students gave up their evening meal to raise more money for the second house. Their fast produced nearly two thousand dollars!

Marist School, a Roman Catholic day school in Atlanta, was the first high school to form a Campus Chapter and Bethel Seminary in St. Paul, Minnesota was the first seminary. Youth involvement in Habitat is exciting, and often energizes adults to become more involved.

The Bishop Dwenger High School Campus Chapter in Fort Wayne, Indiana organized three additional high schools and forty grade schools in the Catholic Diocese there to sponsor and build a Habitat house in 1995. Some thirteen thousand young people raised the $25,000 needed, and teams of thirty students per day, plus their adult supervisors, worked on the construction beginning April 3.

"Teenagers get [too much] praise for athletic achievements, and not enough for service work," said chapter advisor Carl Loesch. "But these young people are leading the adults in this project . . . when young people make the pitch, it's hard for adults to say 'no' to service work."

Habitat truly works at any level as it offers people a chance to give and receive in classic biblical form—the more you give, the more you receive.

Global Village is a perfect case in point.

"A deal is a good deal only if it's a good deal for both sides," is one of our mottos at Habitat. Global Village is surely a "good deal" by that standard because everybody involved benefits from the program.

The program enables volunteers to visit foreign lands at minimal expense, experience different cultures firsthand, and at the same time do something worthwhile.

Global Village works this way: Habitat affiliates, campus chapters, churches, and individuals from Europe, Australia, Japan, Canada, the United States, and other countries organize Global Village work camps to go to Habitat affiliates in developing nations and help build Habitat houses. They work in places as diverse as remote jungle villages, inner-city slums, and poor, dusty country communities. They raise their own travel expenses as well as money for building materials prior to departure.

Every year, hundreds of people spend their own money to join six to thirty others in one- to three-week work camps at international Habitat affiliates. They come to know the people in their chosen country in a way they never could by traveling through as tourists.

In 1994, more than seventy Global Village work camps comprised of some 850 volunteers were sent out all over the world. At least one hundred work camps and one thousand volunteers were projected for 1995. Work camps from all over the country went to such places as Ghana, Nicaragua, Honduras, Guatemala, India, the Philippines, and Tanzania to lay foundations, make concrete bricks, and create houses where there were none before. They returned to tell about the most unusual vacation they'd ever had.

As Claire Richards wrote after returning from her African Global Village Work Camp, "Words cannot even begin to explain what the Zambia trip meant to me. Before, I was locked in a lot of fear regarding life and living. This work camp set me free."

"It profoundly changed my philosophy, making me rethink my priorities. I want to do something constructive and real with my life, not for just one week," wrote Sung Ehn Meng, a high-schooler from Korea after her Global Village Work Camp to the Philippines. "I never want to forget what I learned."

We've seen Global Village take on international twists of its own too. Several Japanese work groups have gone to the Philippines to build Habitat houses. British youth have journeyed to Tanzania in East Africa to build Habitat houses. Likewise, work camps composed of Americans, Australians, and New Zealanders have gone into remote areas of Papua New Guinea to put up Habitat houses. Habitat work groups from the Netherlands have built Habitat houses in Hungary and Tanzania.

Robin Chenoweth and her husband Doral traveled to Ghana after years of regularly volunteering with their Columbus, Ohio affiliate. But their work at home hadn't exactly prepared them for what awaited them in Africa. For two weeks, they lived and worked in villages in southern Ghana with no plumbing and very little electricity, five hours from the nearest telephone. She wrote about her experiences in the Columbus, Ohio *Dispatch*, telling how they showered out of a bucket with cold water and washed their clothes in the river. They also built seven houses—Ghanian style: three rooms, four hundred square feet, concrete floors laid over homemade bricks, with a utility house for the latrine and kitchen.

"Our job was to carry bricks to the site, lay them, and mortar the joints," she wrote. "My Ghanian instructor was a rather brash man named Joseph. He spent hours honing my skills. He later told my husband that he wanted me to be a perfect mason when I returned to the U.S., so I would be a more valuable wife."

As they left, she wrote that she felt a certain guilt. "It was the realization of how lucky we are to be able to leave the poverty and deplorable health conditions behind. It's the realization that will keep us, and all Habitat volunteers, working to end substandard housing around the world and in our corner of the world."[3]

Another exciting new volunteer movement is for "Women Only." The idea originated in Charlotte, North Carolina in 1990 after the prolific affiliate there had dedicated its 100th house. Someone asked, "What can we do for an encore?"

Charlotte Habitat volunteers Darlene Jonas and Ruth Martin answered the question with a question: "Wouldn't we have enough talent to build a house entirely by women?" The rest, as they say, is history. The project was named "Look, Look! See Jane Build!"

A skilled female architect and two women construction professionals took on the responsibility of coordinating the construction and training the volunteers. Women were in charge of every phase, and more than five hundred women became involved in one way or another. Men were allowed on the site only to prepare meals. Rosalynn Carter came for the first day, and my wife Linda was the speaker at the dedication service. Soon Janet—a single mother of two—moved into that special house with her daughters.

Then in Minneapolis, the second all-women-built house went up. Habitat leaders ran a notice in local newspapers, inviting women to come

(Photo by Julie Lopez)

"All together now . . .!" Walls of the W.A.T.C.H. house at Americus, Georgia are ready to go up. (W.A.T.C.H. stands for Women Accepting the Challenge of Housing.)

to a meeting to discuss the idea. The notice said: "It's time for women to put on their aprons and start doing some housework. And we don't mean scrubbing and dusting . . . an all-female team of volunteers will build a house with a low-income woman and her family . . . We're looking for skilled and unskilled women to contribute their labor and for men to contribute childcare and meals . . . This is one form of housework that lasts."

They expected one hundred to one hundred-fifty women to respond; four hundred women showed up! The project was a smash hit!

Soon, all-women projects were going up everywhere. Across the country, projects with such names as Women Helping Women Coalition, W.A.T.C.H. (Women Accepting the Challenge of Housing), The Constructive Women's Project, The Women's House for Habitat, Women Hammer for Habitat, The House that Jill Built, and Belle's Building Brigade popped up in places such as Atlanta, Denver, Austin, San Antonio, Cleveland, Fresno, Houston, and dozens of other cities. In fact, the first house finished in the new Sumter County Initiative to end all poverty housing in our home county was a W.A.T.C.H. house. The third W.A.T.C.H. house in Americus was dedicated in February 1995 in memory of our beloved receptionist, Alberta Moore, who died in December 1994.

Country music artist Reba McEntire sponsored the building of a Nashville "women-only" house in 1994 and showed up to hammer nails with the women volunteers because, she said, she didn't want her involvement to be just "Reba writes a check." In 1995, she sponsored a second house.

Senior Girl Scouts in Greensboro, South Carolina built the first house in the nation sponsored by Girl Scouts. Called the "Gold House," the project earned each of the fifteen young women the Gold Award, the highest achievement of Girl Scouts. It became the 25,001st Habitat house, dedicated just hours after the 25,000th in Charlotte.

Women of the American Legion Auxiliary built one of the houses during the Jimmy Carter Work Project blitz build in Washington, D.C.

New Habitat homeowner Gayle Kinzer shouts for joy at the dedication of her house, much to the delight of sponsor Reba McEntire (far right) and others who were present.

The Sisters of Loretto, a Roman Catholic order of nuns, built an "all-nun" house in connection with their 1994 annual meeting in St. Louis. They plan to make doing so a regular part of their annual gatherings.

A group has even been formed to build the first women-only-built house in the Philippines. Women are making a volunteer difference in Habitat—and they are doing a bang-up job!

Then there are the "RV Gypsies" of Habitat for Humanity, who travel in their recreational vehicles from Habitat site to site to lend helping hands everywhere. The Gypsies were founded by Jack and Lois Wolters of Columbus, North Carolina in 1988 after they tired of the "retiree game," as Jack put it. The RV Gypsies are making a difference wherever they wander, speaking before service groups and churches and appearing on local television stations, working on Habitat houses as they go.

Some people think the Gypsies are nuts to travel hundreds of miles, just to work for free. As Jack Wolters, a former electrical supervisor, answered, "The lure is the joy of fellowship with people who feel as we do. The idea is that the more I give, the more I can give." They've been called the cavalry of Habitat for Humanity. More than 750 members travel the highways, usually in caravans to help local Habitat affiliates.

People from all walks of life are wandering with the RV Gypsies—accountants, ministers, farmers, manufacturers, millwrights, teachers, nurses, credit union managers, and air traffic controllers. They travel in truck campers, tent campers, trailers, and motor homes of all shapes and sizes. Considering that the average age of an RV Gypsy is sixty-five, many people are surprised to see them hoisting shingles and climbing ladders.

When asked why they work with the RV Gypsies, several answered succinctly:

- A retired minister from Ohio said, "After my years of preaching to congregations, I decided that I would spend my retirement in a hands-on ministry."

- Said a bricklayer from Michigan, "We contributed monetarily when we were working, but since we retired, we can work with our hands."

- A retired social services employee from Florida said, "I work for a Jewish Carpenter and my reward is the satisfaction of working with needy people around the country who want to better themselves."

But as RV Gypsy Sandy Dode, who is fifty-three, told a Battle Creek, Michigan reporter, "It doesn't matter how old you are. This is my way of giving back . . . So many of us never think about this when we're young, but it's not a God-given right that I was never cold or hungry." So she now wants to spend her time helping others who are.

Dedicated Habitat volunteer and occasional RV Gypsy Jack Gergen described in a letter the impact on a community made by an RV Gypsy visit:

"Perhaps the most important single factor in the work of the Gypsies," he explained, "is the shot in the arm a one- or two-week visit gives a local affiliate. Even the extra work entailed by such a visit helps solidify the cooperative approach of affiliate members, helpers, and sponsors.

"Out of sheer gratitude for the sudden infusion of volunteers from across the country, the residents of Midland, Michigan banded together to provide lunches and suppers and local tours for the visitors—including good public relations from newspapers, radio, and television media nearly every day.

"Time after time," he continued, "we heard from host representatives that their only previous contact with Habitat for Humanity was in their financial support to the national and worldwide effort. Similarly, we met with local residents whose previous work with Habitat was in far-off blitzes and disaster relief; it appeared to me that the Midland affiliate could logically count on future support from these folks."

The RV Gypsies' crazy lifestyle caught the interest of *Trailer Life Magazine,* and an article by Jim Elder related some of their stories. When Frank Buzzoni's career as an air-traffic controller came to an abrupt halt, he and his wife Diana ultimately found themselves converting their van and becoming RV Gypsies. They have averaged four months on the road each year, mostly for Habitat for Humanity.

After retiring from his California building-trades supply business, Ron Ballay and his wife Marnee became involved in repair and clean-up after Hurricane Hugo hit South Carolina. They soon discovered Habitat, bought a forty-foot Class-A motor home, and began living a mostly full-time RV life. To pay for fuel, they have sold pumpkins and Christmas trees in the fall of the year.

Quoting one of the RV Gypsies, the *Trailer Life* article described a synergy that happens with this blending of service and RV life: "We

145

retired, tried the golf and tennis life, and got bored; bought a small RV and traveled; got bored. After a trip to see the fall foliage in Vermont, we realized we could have stayed home, rented a video of autumn in New England, and had as much a sense of being there. Our fancy, fully self-contained RV had isolated us from the very places and people we visited."

But then on an invitation from RV Gypsy friends, they participated in a Habitat project. Afterward, they said they realized that they had gained as much as they had given—including a sense of people and place by working with local volunteers.

After interviewing a few Gypsies, Elder decided to try the life. He and his wife drove their RV to Americus to help out during our 20/20,000 Blitz Build. In his article he confessed to being "terminally infected" with *habititis* while helping to build our 20,000th house, and has signed up for a future Gypsy project on the road.

The guiding lights of the Gypsies, the Wolters, query local affiliates each spring to see where Gypsies are most needed. Then a schedule is sent to all the Gypsy members and sign-ups begin for the coming season. Whether solo or by caravan, the RV Gypsies are a Habitat force for good anywhere they stop.[4]

(Photo by Chris McGranahan)

Habitat RV Gypsies co-leader Jack Wolters at 20/20,000 Blitz Build in Americus, Georgia.

Volunteers from civic clubs are another vital force behind many community Habitat affiliates. Members of the local Rotary and Kiwanis Clubs, Junior Chambers of Commerce (Jaycees), Junior Leagues, Pilot Clubs, and others are truly service organizations in the best sense of the word. They recognize the positive difference Habitat for Humanity can make in their hometowns.

Typical of such involvement is a Rotary Club in Canton, Ohio. They sponsored a Habitat house in 1994 and another in 1995. The club selected a committee of volunteers to work along with Habitat, helping to build houses, but also to provide a playground, cleanup, and safety.

In 1995 a Rotary Club in Harrisonburg, Virginia co-sponsored a Habitat house with the Campus Chapter of James Madison University.

Churches, of course, are Habitat's most natural partners.

Jimmy Carter often says an interesting thing in his talks about churches. He points out that if every church and synagogue would commit to build one or two houses a year, the problem of poverty housing could be delivered a knockout blow. It's true—and churches are responding to the call. In fact, they are such a potential force in our goal of eliminating poverty housing everywhere that we have devised several special ways to reach out to churches to get them involved.

Our Church Relations Department's task is to seek support from the more than 350,000 churches in the United States, 30,000 in Canada, and the many thousands more around the world. It is our goal to stimulate creative new approaches within these churches to help their members see their neighbors differently and to respond positively to help, in the name of Christ.

The department's more immediate goal is to involve at least half the churches in each area where we have a Habitat affiliate by the end of the decade.

Many Habitat affiliates have had extensive church involvement and support, both in money and volunteers. Some have already achieved the goal of support from half of the local churches. In March of 1995, I was in Sarasota, Florida to speak at the dedication of five new Habitat houses in a thirty-two-house subdivision there. Dr. Frank Evans, their church relations chairman, proudly told me that fifty-one of the 102 churches in the city were currently supporting their work and that their new goal was to have 75 percent of the churches supporting them within two years. Isn't that exciting? That kind of support can be engendered all across the land with continued diligence and hard work.

Consider this: If Habitat could gain the support of half the churches in the United States—that's 175,000 churches—imagine how many houses could be built by that many congregations!

Churches work with Habitat in wonderful, diverse ways. Of course, the simplest and most common form of participation is through contributing money and recruiting volunteers to build houses. Summer work groups are a good way for churches to get involved, and there always are results that reach far beyond the mere construction process.

Few experiences in his church have left a more lasting impression on the people involved, stated Pastor Howard Taylor, than the two summer work groups he led from the First Baptist Church in Woodstown, New Jersey to Habitat projects on Johns Island, South Carolina. As he wrote, "If it is carefully planned, the trip produces an important sense of accomplishing something, even for unskilled people, in a short time. There is the valuable experience of working together to build, in a spirit of Christian fellowship. Lasting friendships are formed and intergenerational understanding increases amazingly. Each time we have taken a work group, they have acquired a fresh sensitivity to the needs of others. This is not limited just to people on the trip. Through fund-raising, prayer vigils, farewell breakfasts at dawn, and welcome-home receptions afterward, the entire congregation gets involved and people are still talking about these trips years later."

Habitat has two exceptional programs created specifically for churches: Adopt-a-House and Covenant Churches.

The term Adopt-a-House is self-explanatory. The congregation does it all, from covering the building expenses to recruiting volunteers to swinging the hammers.

Covenant churches, in an annually renewable written commitment, pledge to pray for Habitat's ministry, contribute financially, and furnish volunteers. Beyond that, each church defines its own commitment based on its particular capabilities and interests. In turn, Habitat promises to carefully manage the money, volunteers, time, and other donated resources.

Some of the suggestions we give for ways churches can keep their Habitat "covenant" include:

- organizing work parties to help build houses for the local affiliate

- selecting a board member to be active in the local affiliate

- supporting "Vision/Habitat," which collects used eyeglasses for Habitat headquarters to ship overseas to meet the need for low-cost eyeglasses and help raise funds from the sale of the eyeglasses to build more houses

- holding an Extraordinary Gift Fair offering church members the opportunity to "purchase" construction supplies to build houses as "extraordinary" gift-giving

- celebrating the International Day of Prayer and Action for Human Habitat on the third Sunday of September every year.

Church youth groups make terrific partners. Twenty-five high schoolers from St. John's Baptist Church in Charlotte, North Carolina wanted to tackle a mission job at home. So they attended training sessions on house construction and raised $32,500 by doing yard work and other odd jobs around town. They stayed in the dormitory at a local college, began working on the house at daybreak, and virtually had the house built by week's end.

Youth group Habitat work camps are a summer fixture in some churches. The First Presbyterian Church in Metuchen, New Jersey has sent groups of adults and youth traveling to work on Habitat projects for several years. The first year they went to repair inner-city houses in Hartford, Connecticut. The second year, they reconstructed a condemned house in northern Vermont. For two years in a row, they took youth groups to work in Circleville, West Virginia, a gorgeous area of the country with some of the nation's worst poverty. The teens gained valuable insight into how people in different circumstances live, while learning building skills.

Sunday schoolers at Asbury United Methodist Church in Salisbury, Maryland decided to help Habitat by collecting a mile of pennies. Estimating it would take 87,500 pennies (equal to $875), the children took Habitat banks home with them and began saving pennies wherever they found them. After several months, they totaled the pennies and presented them in two wheelbarrows to a Habitat representative during their church service. By the time all those pennies were pooled together and counted, they had collected $1,176.69—that's 117,669 pennies—spanning 1.34 miles!

Catholic youth from five states blitz-built four houses in Denver, Colorado in anticipation of Pope John Paul II's visit as a part of World Youth Day in 1994.

First Congregational Church in Kent, Connecticut opened a thrift shop as a means of raising money for needs in their community and chose to use some of the earnings to build Habitat houses in Ghana.

Many churches are in direct partnerships with our international work. The longest partnership of this kind is with Plymouth Congregational Church in Plymouth, New Hampshire. When we started building houses back in 1974 in Zaire, Plymouth Congregational was first in line to give the two thousand dollars required to build a house. Ultimately, the church was instrumental in setting up a statewide affiliate organization as well as a local affiliate.

Often, a whole group of churches will come together to build a Habitat house. For instance, in the spring of 1995, twenty-three churches comprising the Parish of the Evangelical Lutheran Church in America and six Roman Catholic churches in the San Jose Catholic Diocese joined hands to sponsor the tenth Habitat house in partnership with Bay and Valley Habitat for Humanity located in Santa Clara County, California.

A little town in Illinois also shows how churches find common ground with Habitat, and beautifully underscores the theology of the hammer. In Gridley, individuals from various churches had worked together on community projects, yet churches rarely cooperated with each other. But the little Habitat house built in Gridley changed that. Over several months, United Methodists, Roman Catholics, Lutherans, Disciples of Christ, Apostolic Christians, and Mennonites worked together to get the job done.

In Brunswick, Georgia, the Habitat affiliate believes that church support is the secret to success. In 1995, the affiliate planned to build twelve houses, with eight sponsored by churches. In Canton, Ohio, the Habitat affiliate blitz-built seven houses in July 1995 to celebrate their seventh anniversary. Six of the houses were sponsored by churches.

Sometimes working with Habitat for Humanity can actually revitalize a church. A wonderful story to illustrate this concerns St. Andrew's Episcopal Church in Kansas City, Missouri, which was a church in trouble in the early '80s, even though it was the largest and wealthiest church in its diocese.

A heated dispute had left the church politically divided and emotionally distressed. Attendance had plummeted to one-fourth its membership, and the rector was asked to resign. Things were not good. Today, the church is energetic, active, and enjoying a spiritual renewal—and the church's work with Kansas City Habitat for Humanity gets some of the credit. "The new rector," as one of the church's members put it, "had this crazy idea that we should get involved with Habitat for Humanity and build a house as a way to celebrate the parish's seventy-fifth birthday. Habitat was an important factor in helping us get healthy again."

Jeff Black, the rector, explained it this way: "When I first came to St. Andrew's, I realized the church had needed to be more involved in ministries of compassion and outreach. Habitat is one program where people can act out a change of heart." Building their first house was such a good experience, they soon were planning ways to build a house each year. Soon, seven families in the Kansas City area owned Habitat houses sponsored by St. Andrew's. The church also helped another local housing program by providing more families with homes.

Attendance is now up at St. Andrew's, parishioners are involved in new forms of worship, and home Bible study groups and choir members have formed volunteer crews to work on Habitat sites themselves. They've also begun to reach out to other congregations and started recognizing the poor among them by inviting them in.

Even entire denominations have gotten caught up in the excitement. In October 1989, the Home Mission Board of the Southern Baptist Convention sponsored a Habitat house with the Atlanta affiliate. In June 1993, in the first such event conducted in connection with a national gathering of the denomination, more than fifty builders from the General

Assembly of the Presbyterian Church USA came days early for their annual meeting to help blitz build four Habitat houses in Orlando, Florida.

But as for pure energy and creativity, I'm constantly amazed at what just one person, with whatever talent he or she has, can do. A finely trained musician who had gone overseas to help our international effort one day realized he could certainly do more for Habitat with his hands than just swing a hammer. He began giving piano concerts, charging a small admission which went to Habitat for Humanity. Numerous bicyclists have crisscrossed the United States and Canada, raising money and helping build Habitat houses. And one man literally gave himself, climbing up on a billboard and vowing to remain there until enough money, labor, and materials for four houses were contributed. Six days later, under a tornado threat, he came down—after raising sixty thousand dollars. His successful stunt inspired another man to do the same thing for his city's affiliate in another state.

One proof of Habitat for Humanity's power to infuse volunteers with continuing enthusiasm is the fact that the older affiliates are doing so well. People are not running out of steam. They're just as excited now as fifteen to eighteen years ago—a phenomenon that seems impossible when you think about the normally high drop-out rate of volunteers.

But it's true. San Antonio, Texas, the first city to have an affiliate outside of Georgia, continues building houses. In fact, its tempo of building is steadily increasing. Immokalee, Florida Habitat started soon after San Antonio. They have built more than one hundred houses and expect to double that number within the next few years.

The Kansas City, Missouri Habitat affiliate, begun in October 1979, set a goal to build fifty houses by 1989. They did that, and will be well past one hundred houses by the year 2000. The story is the same all over the country. Some affiliates build faster than others. Some prefer blitz campaigns. Others just work steadily, week after week, getting the job done. Of course, there are discouragements, setbacks, and very real disappointments. Sometimes there are financial shortages. Sometimes there are leadership problems. But they all keep going and the new homeowners work hard for their new future along with all those volunteers who get paid in ways far beyond monetary remuneration. Of course, all those efforts result in more and more simple, decent houses going up every single day.

Sometimes volunteers' stories have power all their own, and they are unforgettable. I'd like to share with you two of those stories in the volunteer's own words, written for our newspaper, *Habitat World.* The two individuals are Tom Schmidt, a former *Milwaukee Journal* reporter, and Willie Wilkerson, a volunteer with the Atlanta affiliate since 1983.

> "Habitat changed my life in a very real sense because it resurrected my heart, spirit, and soul. Although I was raised in a Spirit-based family, I'd been leading a fairly narrow but pleasant secular life. I had a relatively meaningless and draining job at the *Journal* writing about housing for rich people.
>
> I found the job especially disturbing after the Jimmy Carter Work Project. Habitat opened me up to the possibility of a different way of living. But the paper wouldn't let me join the local Habitat affiliate. They felt it would be a potential conflict of interest. If I joined Habitat, I would be reassigned. Usually that meant covering night meetings in the suburbs. So I quit.
>
> Today, Terese and I live in Victor, Idaho. I'm a freelance travel writer. Terese is a nurse. One of the benefits we've gained through Habitat involvement was totally unexpected: it gave us building skills to build our own house last summer. With the money we've saved by doing that, we volunteer at other blitz builds. Terese swings a twenty-four-ounce framing hammer with great authority.
>
> Habitat is the spiritual center of my life. I can't listen to a sermon, prayer, or Scripture reading without thinking of Habitat. I feel God's presence at every project."
>
> —*Tom Schmidt*[5]

"Every day of my life is Habitat for Humanity. I love to tell people about it, and I try to rub it off on others. I wear my Habitat cap and tee shirt to work and some days two or three different people will ask me about Habitat. I tell them that Habitat is love in action through partnership. I have been a volunteer for ten years now. I read an article about Habitat when I was laid up after an accident and I decided to get involved. From the first Saturday in 1983 when I worked on a house with the Atlanta affiliate, I was sold on it.

As I grow older, I become more involved. Volunteering with Habitat has helped me to grow and has made my life rewarding and enjoyable.

I teach a construction class at the South Fulton Vocational School in College Park, a suburb of Atlanta. . . . I take them to work on Habitat sites. I teach them how much can be accomplished when you work together as a team, whether or not you're getting paid for it.

My wife and thirteen-year-old son came with me to the 20/20,000 Blitz Build in Americus. My wife, Joyce, said that the project helped to put more love in her. "These people are all in one," she said. Watching my family in Americus made me feel thirty feet tall. This project was beautiful. No, it was *beyond* beautiful. Habitat has changed my life in many ways. I have learned that anything can be accomplished when people work together."

—*Willie Wilkerson*[6]

In so many endeavors in life, someone has to be the winner and someone the loser: athletic contests, elections, promotions. But with Habitat for Humanity, you're engaging in an activity that uplifts you and everyone around you. Habitat is a win/win/win/win deal for everybody involved. It's a win for the homeowner partners. It's a win for the volunteer partners. It's a win for the donor partners. And it's a win for the community, the nation, and the world.

How many opportunities in life can boast that? It is perhaps the special secret of "infectious habititis," and may it spread, spread, spread! Thousands of dedicated volunteers are making it happen.

CHAPTER EIGHT

Why Build for the Rest of the World?

Habitat's International Work

THE INTERNATIONAL work always has been a part of the vision of Habitat for Humanity. This ministry started in the small Christian community of Koinonia in southwest Georgia, but it moved next to Zaire in Central Africa.

There are those people, however, who don't want to support anything outside the United States. "Why should we build houses for the rest of the world? We have too many problems right here at home," they say.

It is true that we have huge problems throughout the United States. So, how can we justify our work in other countries?

First of all, it is sound religion to be concerned about the whole world. God is not an American citizen. His love is universal. One of my favorite scriptures is John 3:16: "For God so loved the *world* that He gave His only begotten Son that whoever believes in Him should not perish but have everlasting life" (NKJV). If God's love has no limits, then our love expressed through the work of Habitat for Humanity should likewise have no limits.

Second, we should be thinking about enlightened self-interest too. Our world today is one of instant global communication. Even the poorest villages in the most remote areas of the world have access to news from everywhere via satellite transmissions. These people know that the standard of living in the United States is vastly higher than where they live, and many are making plans constantly on how to get here. So if Habitat accomplishes what we have set out to do in the U.S.—that is, eliminate substandard housing—then that becomes an increasing attraction to people who are tempted to leave home for a place where there is the chance for a better life.

But the truth is that most people would really prefer to stay where they are if they can have a decent life there. They don't like to pull up and leave friends and family and familiar languages and familiar customs and go off to a foreign land they know nothing about. They leave their homeland out of desperation. Things are so bad that they are willing to risk their lives to get to a richer country that offers a better life. So just as a practical matter, we should help make life better for people where they are—so they don't feel compelled to come to the United States. The reality is, beyond the Statue of Liberty's wonderfully American statement—"Give me your tired and your poor . . . your huddled masses yearning to breathe free"—is that the United States cannot accept the billions of people around the world who might wish to migrate here. We must help people have a simple, decent place to live right where they are—and thereby help them stay there.

Third, I feel very strongly that God's mandate for this ministry is worldwide in scope. God's call to us, if you will, is to go *into all the world,* and incarnate His love by building and renovating houses so people everywhere will have, at the very least, *a simple, decent place to live.* I believe this very strongly and am convinced that we are acting in full accord with God's will as we expand our work across the land and all around the world.

It is for these three very fundamental reasons that we work in other countries. We cannot live in splendid isolation and pretend that the rest of the world does not exist. There are people who would like to do that, but I'm not one of them. We need to help people where they are in the United States and in other nations too.

As of late 1995, we are building thousands of Habitat houses in the United States in more than twelve hundred affiliates. Furthermore, new U.S. Habitat affiliates are continually being formed all over the country at the rate of ten to fifteen each month. Most of the affiliates, both old and new, are building more and more houses each year. But we can—and should—build elsewhere too. Habitat for Humanity currently has affiliates in forty-six countries, building houses in more than seven hundred locations. I'd say that within two years we will be in at least fifty countries, building in more than one thousand locations. The ultimate intention is to establish Habitat for Humanity in every nation on earth. That's one hundred ninety-one countries.

All local Habitat affiliates in the United States, Canada, Australia, New Zealand, the United Kingdom, Poland, Hungary, and all other countries are expected to give 10 percent of the money raised locally for building houses in developing countries. Note that I said *all* countries. We encourage even the poorest Habitat affiliates in the poorest countries to help other poor people in other countries. No Habitat affiliate anywhere should be denied the blessing of giving to help others.

Linda and I lived in Zaire for three years—from 1973 to 1976— and started 114 houses in Mbandaka, the capital city of Equator Region. Then we went to the southern part of the region and started three hundred more houses. In July 1995, we went back to Zaire to celebrate the Twentieth Anniversary of Habitat for Humanity in that country. We had built nearly two thousand houses there, despite political turmoil and trouble. From personal experience, having lived in that developing country, I know what the need is, so I am very personally committed to the worldwide work of Habitat for Humanity.

Houses are being built everywhere. For instance, consider the following:

- The 2,000th house was built in India in 1994. Less than two years earlier, Linda and I helped dedicate the 1,000th house in that country, a milestone that took ten years to achieve.

- More than a thousand Habitat houses have been built throughout six locations in the Philippines.

- Under the leadership of National Coordinator Sefatiya Mboneraho, Uganda Habitat for Humanity recently celebrated the completion of its 1,200th house since affiliating in 1980. That number is projected to double in two years.

- In October 1994, a grand celebration was held in Nicaragua marking the completion of one thousand Habitat houses in that war-torn land.

- In all of Latin America and the Caribbean, sixty-one active affiliates have completed ten thousand houses.

- In the Mezquital Valley, ninety miles north of Mexico City, one thousand houses were built in fifty villages in one year alone.

- In Peru, where more than six hundred houses a year are being built, the excitement about Habitat for Humanity is fantastic. The board of directors of Habitat for Humanity International met in Arequipa, Peru several years ago, followed by a tour of Habitat affiliates in Arequipa, Juliaca, Puno, and Vila-Vila. Everywhere we went, we were met by hundreds of Habitat homeowners, prospective homeowners, and friends throwing confetti and flowers, yelling and waving, so full of enthusiasm that they could barely contain themselves.

Building Habitat houses helps make a difference with other problems in these countries too. Scott Mulrooney, an International Partner in Guatemala, wrote about the real difference Habitat is making in his adopted country, racially, religiously, and sociologically—one house, one family at a time.

"Habitat Guatemala has the privilege of serving as a bridge of unity in the communities where we partner," he explains. "This bridging manifests itself in three manners. First, ever since 1492, the indigenous Mayans have struggled with the Spanish colonialists. This five-hundred-year-old struggle continues still today both passively and often times violently. But through Habitat, *Indigenas* and *Ladinos* work side by side sweating, laughing, sharing, and building bonds of peace and houses of hope.

"However," he admits, "though we may be able to create trust and understanding between families, we still struggle to overcome military oppression against community organizing and empowerment of the poor.

"Another clash that is typical to Guatemala is the division between various religions," he goes on. "Certainly there exist grand differences between the Mayan religions and Christianity, or even between the

(Photo by Julie Lopez)

Habitat's work in Guatemala brings new hope to many families in need.

conservative Catholic church and its own branch of Liberation theology. But the main cause for separation lies between Catholicism and Protestantism. And here once again Habitat bridges this gap between neighbors with *Catolicos* and *Evangelicos* developing respect for each other as they build together."

Perhaps one of the most tangible results of Habitat's work, he says, is battling one of the strongest cultural forces shaping Guatemala and the rest of Latin America in the modern word. "Since World War II, the rural population of Guatemala has been making a mass exodus into the urban centers, primarily the capital." Fifty years ago, he explains, over 90 percent of Guatemalans lived in rural areas; now half live in the cities. "Needless to say, urban districts are not prepared to absorb such rapid growth. Thus, the majority of these tenacious immigrants collect themselves into spontaneous or squatter settlements, often illegally occupying invaded land." They hope for a better life, he writes, to break the cycle of poverty that is part of rural living, but what they find is often worse than what they left. "By providing simple, decent housing to rural dwellers for whom there exists no other option for obtaining a decent home, Habitat is removing at least one of the reasons that push inhabitants to leave their farming communities."

What's it like building in other countries? "Dull" is not a word you'd ever use to describe it. In fact, there is plenty of excitment. Working in foreign lands, you never know what to expect.

A few years ago, at a Habitat site in Uganda, our dump truck was commandeered by an army commander in the area. The officer decided he needed the nice truck more than our workers did. After being unable to regain the truck through normal channels, we asked Jimmy Carter to contact the president of Uganda. Within a few days the truck was returned, and the officer was reprimanded.

(Photo by Julie Lopez)

Habitat homeowner-to-be mixes cement at the village of San Juan Ostuncalco, Guatemala.

A tragedy occurred in South Africa. In Alexandra, an enclave of Johannesburg—in a no-man's-land dubbed by the warring factions as "no-go zone"—Habitat was building several houses. The land was readily available . . . because no one else wanted it. Living there was too dangerous. Habitat had been able to build nineteen houses before the political violence set in again. Many people were scared away from the area—so many that Habitat was forced to shut down for a few months. Then in June 1992, work resumed.

One day in December 1992, several men and women were putting in sweat equity on Norah Mchunu's house in order to qualify for their own house. The director of the affiliate already had told his volunteers that no one had to go back to work if they didn't want to. But these volunteers kept on working, especially two women—Norah, the homeowner, and her friend Lizzy Nkosi.

A car came by slowly. Two men got out of the car and came toward the volunteers working on the house. The male volunteers, seeing that the two men were armed, ran for cover. But Lizzy and Norah believed since they were women—and since they were working on Habitat ground—they would be safe. That is how much they wanted their own homes. Instead, the men opened fire, mistaking the women for political rivals. The two women were shot repeatedly—Lizzy eleven times and Norah eighteen. The last bullet hit a coin Lizzy had tucked in her bra, over her heart. Both lived, but were hospitalized for months.

Norah's house was finally finished and she now lives there. Lizzy has her sweat equity hours completed but she refuses to live in the area. "I will wait for other land," she was quoted as saying in a *Boston Globe* article, "but meanwhile, I will help others to build their homes."

We've even built in Northern Ireland. I visited there in January 1993 with Tom Jones, director of our Washington, D.C. office, to plant the seeds for Habitat's work. In inner-city Belfast, most Catholics and Protestants live in polarized communities separated by so-called "peacelines"—walls that separate people who have lived in fear of one another for years. Over the past twenty-five years, the government has provided good public housing in Belfast, addressing the physical needs—but has been unable to affect a change in the human problem of the divided communities. Habitat wanted to try to help do just that. Habitat for Humanity in Northern Ireland is a "cross-community Christian initiative," challenged to build with both communities in an effort to break down the traditional barriers. Thoughtful research went into choosing just the right site in the Catholic and Protestant areas for Habitat's first project, because being accepted by the community was of utmost importance. The site finally selected was in the Catholic community of Iris Close Estate, an area of extreme urban deprivation and suspicion.

In May 1994, eighteen American students from Villanova University in Pennsylvania laid foundations for two houses and laid an even deeper foundation in the hearts of the people. Their hard work and enthusiasm drew unusual local support. Because of a suspicion of outsiders, getting local volunteers was not easy. But by appealing to those who sincerely desired reconciliation, Habitat attracted people of different backgrounds who were willing to risk entering an area that previously they would never have dared enter. "As someone from 'Loyalist' East Belfast, it was exciting to work with Habitat in West Belfast, a perceived Nationalist heartland," said Irish volunteer Alan George. "In carrying bricks and drinking tea together, you live out a politic that goes beyond rhetoric and tradition, a politic dealing with the basic needs of ordinary people— a place to live, a place to make friends, and an opportunity to discover again all that we have in common, rather than be reminded about what supposedly divides us."

Sadly, the second homeowner chosen for the project was murdered only weeks before the blitz build. However, the effort continues, and as more houses go up, hope is high. The threat of violence is everywhere in this city, yet the Habitat affiliate believes their work is making a difference.[1]

Sometimes we've been forced by local conditions to temporarily evacuate our International Partners. In 1981, International Partners were called home from Guatemala because of mounting unrest. We did not send volunteers there again until 1984. But despite difficulties that slowed or stopped the work, within two years more than one hundred families had moved from mostly cornstalk and mud huts to solid, earthquake-resistant homes. Since then, more than eighteen hundred houses have been built and new ones are currently going up at the rate of fifty a month.

Does an idea like Habitat for Humanity have the power to bring people together even after years of in-fighting and civil war? I believe it does. On the community level, people breaking out of their usual circles find those they encounter in the next circle are not that different from them. This interaction between groups and individuals with diverse backgrounds is in the best tradition of the theology of the hammer. We're trying it in Northern Ireland, we're trying it in South Africa, we're trying it in Guatemala . . . and elsewhere.

One of the most hopeful situations is in El Salvador. The national committee in that country includes people from the "right" and the "left." In the group are people who had been aligned during their civil war with the guerrillas and with the army. Now, they've come together to build houses. So Habitat is working hard to make dangerous places safe in its own peacemaking way—using the power of the hammer.

Two different programs fuel our international effort: Global Village and International Partners.

The Global Village program, as explained in the previous chapter, involves sending out work camp groups to these international sites for a period of one or more weeks. These groups come in all shapes, sizes, and origins—from church groups to campus groups to corporate groups. Each year the opportunities are planned, printed in our newspaper *Habitat World,* and widely announced for volunteers to respond. In 1994 overseas work camps went out to build Habitat houses in Botswana, Brazil, the Dominican Republic, Ethiopia, Guatemala, Hungary, Papua New Guinea, the Philippines, Uganda, and Zambia.

International Partners are those who have been trained in Americus at headquarters to serve with Habitat for Humanity in other countries. Most of them are assigned to Habitat sites in developing countries for a period of time—usually three years. Habitat for Humanity provides a stipend allowing for a simple, healthy lifestyle in the community where they will serve.

The work isn't easy. International Partners spend seven weeks in training, followed by one or two months of fund-raising and speaking engagements prior to departure. Training provides instruction in the duties usually required of any International Partner in his or her adopted land, including developing culturally appropriate systems of construction and training people in such mundane but essential tasks as bookkeeping. Whatever expertise potential International Partners have, they will use—plus new skills they never knew they could acquire. The dedication and ambition of an International Partner takes mountains of faith, dedication, compassion, and strong character. Incidentally, not all International Partners are Americans. We have had partners from Canada, Mexico, the Netherlands, Germany, Australia, Brazil, and other countries.

Papua New Guinea is one of the countries where our work is going strong. Two women—Nancy Cardwell, then editor of *Habitat World* who led a Global Village Work Camp to Papua New Guinea, and Donna

(Photo by Bryan Bargen)

The climate and landscape of Papua New Guinea prompt the building of Habitat houses on stilts to protect them from the elements.

Minich, who had worked there as an International Partner and is now database manager at Habitat headquarters—are articulate in describing their slice-of-life experiences in Habitat's international work.

Nancy loved to travel. So when Habitat's Global Village Department asked her if she wanted to help lead a work camp to Papua New Guinea, she said, "Yes." It didn't matter that she knew only vaguely that Papua New Guinea was somewhere in the South Pacific or that guidebooks emphasized its primitive living conditions and nonexistent amenities. It is a country that occupies half a large island just north of Australia. It has few roads and most of the four million people live in rural villages so remote that the small country has more than seven hundred local languages. Still, she was ready to go.

"I didn't know I was headed for one of the most rewarding experiences of my life," she said. Their work camp included fourteen Papua New Guineans and nine Americans. The work camp's time and efforts were divided among five villages.

"We learned of our roving itinerary shortly after we arrived in Maruruo, in the northern part of the country. The nine Americans on the trip had traveled five days to reach this beautiful mountaintop village. The thought of leaving it—and repeatedly packing our overstuffed luggage—was disheartening at first." By the end of the trip, she said they were rejoicing in their good fortune.

"In each village—from the heights of Maruruo where we saw the moon rise through the clouds below us, to the shores of Katika where we bathed in a freshwater lagoon—we were warmly welcomed by our hosts. We carried timber through the jungle together, prayed in their churches, and lived in their homes.

"In Maruruo, we carried timber for the eleventh and twelfth Habitat houses there. In Masangko (which we reached by a two-and-a-half-hour slog along a muddy trail through the rain forest) we raised the walls on the fifth and tenth houses. And in Katika, we inaugurated Habitat's work by blitz-building the first house there."

Traditional houses, she explained, have walls of hand-hewn boards or woven bamboo, with bamboo floors and palm roofs. Smoke and insects are big health hazards. "But the people in Habitat houses are healthier and safer, and they don't get sick," her Masangko host told her.

"When we arrived at each village, we were greeted by a traditional sing-sing celebration," she went on. "Frightening-looking men with painted faces and feathered headdresses chanted and danced to the beat of lizard-covered kundu drums. By our last night in Katika, we were wearing headdresses and dancing with them. As we departed Kamamu, a woman who had been traveling with us said tearfully, 'I know you will come back. Next time, you will come to my village.'"[2]

When Donna Minich, her husband David, and their children arrived in Papua New Guinea as International Partners for their three-year stint of service, the first thing they encountered was a murder. A son of the Habitat committee chairman in Kusip, where they were assigned, had been killed in a brawl by someone from another village. In a land where traditions of tribal feuds and cultural differences have long ruled the ways of the people, revenge is a given. Donna knew the cycle well. If the man's son was avenged with a death, then someone from their village would be killed to avenge that death and it would never end.

Soon, she learned about the seven hundred indigenous languages spoken by the population. Each language group consists of a cluster of villages called *tok ples,* or "the language place." By tradition, people from other areas are considered treacherous enemies. Only *wantoks,* or people who speak the same language, should be associated with or helped.

"When we arrived in 1987," she explained, "we found ourselves in the midst of this volatile tribal crisis. Fortunately, after discussion among the village 'headmen,' reason prevailed and the murder of the Habitat committee chairman's son was never avenged."

But the mentality of the people was a problem. Whenever they talked to "outsiders" about Habitat's work, they would face verbal attacks from the Kusip committee.

"The villagers would shout angrily at David: 'You belong to us, this work belongs to us. We don't want to share you or the houses!' Though it wasn't easy, David explained that God wanted all people to have good houses, not just *wantoks,* or people from one *tok ples.* But as Habitat built more houses, local understanding of Habitat grew—as did indigenous pride in the work being accomplished."

Soon, Donna explained, the people were willing to host other villagers who wanted to see the work first-hand. Locals welcomed guests with food and shelter which was an unprecedented practice for treating out-siders. Things were changing. One dramatic change of heart by an important villager started it all.

"The crossing of cultural barriers began in 1989 when Lampu, the local village headman, volunteered to work in a different *tok ples.* As Lampu led the way in helping to build a stranger's house, the villagers began to *helpim helpim*—to help one another, rather than helping only *wantoks,*" she said.

"Today, the people accept that if the work is for Habitat, the old tradi-tion of clan violence does not apply. In fact, a new tradition of work camps, or *bung wik* (a week of gathering together), has caught on throughout the land. During *bung wik,* people from all over the country gather in the host-ing area to blitz-build houses together," Donna said.

In the twelve years that Habitat has been in Papua New Guinea, it has grown to five affiliates covering nearly fifty communities that have built more than five hundred houses. In 1995, the first National Assembly involving delegates from all Papua New Guinea affiliates was formed. Increasingly, Habitat's work is helping to break down thousands of years of violence through *helpim helpim.*[3]

How do international affiliates start?

There are many ways.

A couple of years ago I received a telephone call from Jimmy Carter. He said, "I have Dr. Cheddi Jagen in my office. He's the new president of Guyana, the first democratically elected president of his country. I've told him about Habitat for Humanity. He would like to have Habitat in Guyana. Could you come over to talk to him?" So I grabbed Dick Perry, then director of our work in Latin America, and we drove to the Carter Center to meet Dr. Jagen.

"I would like to see Habitat for Humanity come to Guyana," he told us. "The president's office is open to you. Just let me know how I can be helpful."

In mid-1994, Charlie and Ruth Magill, International Partners who had recently completed a very successful term of service in Guatemala, were assigned to Guyana to help start the work there.

How Habitat for Humanity is getting started in Guyana is quite typical of how we start in any new country. To be sure, we seldom hear directly from the president, but *somebody* will contact us—either a citizen of the country or someone working or visiting there.

They've read one of my books, heard me speak somewhere, read an article about Jimmy Carter's involvement with Habitat for Humanity, or seen a television program about Habitat. They write or phone and say, "I'm a missionary in Belize," or, "I'm working in Nepal," or, "I take business trips to this or that country. I really want to help and I believe in Habitat for Humanity. Do you have any work there? If you don't, could you tell me how to start it?"

There are a multitude of ways that people in various countries learn about Habitat for Humanity. Earlier, I mentioned the *Reader's Digest* article. Literally thousands of people from all over the world wrote to us as a result of that article. We even heard from a New Zealand couple, Neville and Fiona Eastwood, who came to the United States to work

(Habitat for Humanity file photo)

The "Irish Brigade," a work camp group from Northern Ireland, at a Habitat site in Homestead, Florida.

with us after reading about the ministry in *Reader's Digest*. They worked in Georgia, Florida, California, and several other places before returning to New Zealand to continue working with Habitat there.

A good example of how the overseas work begins is the new affiliate in Northern Ireland. The young Irish couple running the program heard Tony Campolo speak in London. He talked about Habitat for Humanity. Peter Farquharson and his wife Jane were living there at that time. They were inspired to move to Americus, Georgia and serve as volunteers for three months at our Habitat headquarters. Now they're directing Habitat's work in Northern Ireland.

Jimmy and Rosalynn Carter have consistently been strong supporters of our international efforts. On his frequent trips around the world, Jimmy Carter takes time to visit Habitat projects and make personal contacts with Habitat leaders.

In Nicaragua, he rode for hours on rough roads to visit a Habitat project in a far corner of the country. By the side of the president of Nicaragua, he laid blocks and attended the dedication of several Habitat homes. In Peru, he helicoptered to a Habitat site high in the Andes Mountains. Two of the Jimmy Carter Work Projects have been international ones, in Mexico and Canada. The 1996 Jimmy Carter Work Project is scheduled to take place in Hungary.

Habitat for Humanity Canada celebrated its Tenth Anniversary in 1995 during the Fiftieth Anniversary of the United Nations. As of mid-1995 there were twenty-six local affiliates in seven provinces and another thirty affiliates in the process of formation. In such a cold climate, a warm, decent place to live is essential to survival.

During the 1993 Jimmy Carter Work Project held in Kitchener, Ontario and Winnipeg, Manitoba, Ed Schreyer—former Premier of Manitoba and Canada's governor-general and commander-in-chief from 1979 to 1984—caught the Habitat spirit. In the summer of '94 while the Jimmy Carter Work Project was in progress in South Dakota, Habitat Canada embarked on a cross-country—from sea to shining sea—building blitz stretching from the Atlantic to the Pacific. The Ed Schreyer "Homes Across Canada Tour" involved two thousand volunteers, and more than forty-five national sponsors building houses for fifteen families in eleven communities.

Deborah Gambriel of Windsor, Ontario was one of the proud homeowners. During the first week her family spent in their new Habitat home, her six-year-old daughter yelled from the bathroom that she could see through the bath water to the bottom of the tub. In their old house, the water was so dirty that it was not fit to drink or bathe in. It had no potable water, a leaky roof, and no insulation from the Canada cold. "We are looking forward to winter and not having to wear our coats, mitts, and boots in the house because of the cold," she said. "We won't have to stay at other people's homes to keep warm."[4]

Though the challenges for affiliates overseas are different than those in North America, they can sometimes be much more overwhelming. Factor in fragile economies, endemic inflation, and civil war, and even the most worthy of social programs can suffer.

But Habitat seems to meet the challenges, sometimes in very creative ways. For example, in 1994 Habitat completed more than 170 houses in

Zaire, a country torn by civil unrest, where cement prices rose so high that house costs quadrupled to four thousand dollars each. So what did the affiliates do? They taught homeowners how to make clay tiles to replace cement floors and tin roofs. In areas where clay was available, this idea reduced the cost of houses to less than one thousand dollars each.

Homeowners in nations with fragile economies are often faced with the challenge of making their house payments. For some homeowners in Khammam, India, the answer was to make payments in bags of grain that were stored in a local church. When grain prices rose high enough, committee members would sell the grain and pay the homeowners' monthly mortgage payments out of the proceeds.[5]

Creativity. That's what is called for. One creative answer is Heifer Project International, one of the nonprofit organizations with which we are happy partners.

"One of the biggest problems Habitat faces in Africa is that the people are so poor, there's no way for them to be able to afford even the small payments required for a Habitat house," states Harry Goodall, Habitat's Area Director for Africa. "That's why Heifer Project is such a fantastic complement to Habitat."

Ruth Cudjoe stood in front of her Ghana Habitat house with her family's cow and proudly posed for a picture to illustrate the project that has helped her so much. She and her two children are participants in the special partnership between Habitat for Humanity and Heifer Project International. Her cow is not only their vital source of nutritious milk, but the cow is literally the family's "mortgage payments on the hoof."

The average annual income for a family of six in Ghana is about five hundred dollars, barely more than forty dollars per month. Employment is limited to subsistence farming and small cottage industries. For families struggling to feed and clothe themselves, the five-dollar monthly payment for a Habitat house may be too high a price to pay.

Now in its fiftieth year, Heifer Project International provides struggling families with livestock and agricultural training. In addition to providing the family with needed food, the income from the sale of meat, eggs, milk, or offspring makes it possible for families to afford school fees for children, medicine when illness strikes, and—most importantly—a simple, decent place to live. Incidentally, Ruth named her cow "Nso Nyame ye," which means "nothing is impossible with God."[6]

An important step in strengthening our international work occurred in July 1994, when fourteen of Habitat's key international leaders came to the United States to participate in "Global Leadership 2000." The program was an intensive, two-week forum focusing on how to connect overseas partners with Habitat leaders in the U.S. As we expand in various countries around the world, we are encouraging Habitat leaders to form national boards. "Global Leadership 2000" was held to talk about how to form these national groups and how, as an organization, to become a "borderless worldwide Habitat for Humanity," not simply a U.S. program with some work in other countries.

Habitat for Humanity has a goal to build more than ten thousand homes outside the United States in 1996. It will happen. The need is great, but the desire and commitment are greater still.

What is it like to work in a developing country for Habitat for Humanity International?

I know of no better way to let you know than to give you a peek into the journals of two of our International Partners:

> Friday, I wake up at 5:30 A.M., drink a cup of coffee, and read *My Utmost for His Highest* by Oswald Chambers.
>
> At 6:00 A.M., I tutor a homeowner in mathematics and physics.
>
> At 7:00 A.M., I prepare for and teach math and physics classes at the local high school. At 9:00 A.M., I drive to Essiaman community for a day of Habitat work. Today the homeowners are raising walls on a main house block. The men mix mortar as the women carry sand, water, and blocks. Since I have not mastered carrying heavy objects on my head, I join the men in their work. At the end of the day, I meet with community leaders before I head back to Asikuma. At home, I quickly bathe and leave for fellowship.
>
> At 6:30 P.M., I eat supper—fufu and groundnut soup. As the sun

sets, I head to town for a church service of worship and praise. As the clock strikes 9:00 P.M., I am home.

Good night.

—*Robin Tilghman*
Asikuma, Ghana, West Africa

It is not easy to adopt new attitudes toward time and scheduling. It is not easy to hold people accountable when you don't know the complex unwritten rules of shame and honor.

It is not easy for people completely new to cash economy to save money. It is not easy to manage lumber production when people can't conceive of keeping records. It is not easy for people to remember to use a level or measure fractions of an inch when prior standards of housing dealt with tree bark and kunai grass.

It is not easy, but this is the real work here, and it requires plenty of patience and insight. The real work is *people* work and is therefore hard to manage neatly and predictably. My sense of mission is to humbly strive to accomplish the above—and much more—in a uniquely Christian context. It is by stretching people in this manner that the building of solid decent homes will hopefully continue long after I'm gone. It can be hard—but it is gratifying.

—*Bill Sitterley*
Lae, Papua New Guinea, South Pacific

Many of the International Partners could write books themselves about their experiences. I've decided to let them tell you what it's like in their own words. Following are several excerpts from letters and reports we've received from International Partners over the years. These speak volumes about the hardships and the joys of building Habitat houses around the world.

Some write about the excitement of their arrival in their new country and of the wonder of the land and people and their many experiences in getting settled there.

On the 12th of January 1995, a very tired and somewhat confused Andrews family disembarked from their plane on a small, tropical island in the Indiana Ocean. Sri Lanka!

The scene on the other side of the wall separating Customs from Sri Lanka was straight out of a movie. Masses of people, many barefoot, stood behind ropes waiting for plane arrivals. Thank goodness, one of them wore shoes and had a smile for our family. Steve Weir, in the country for one year with his family, ushered us out to the street and to a waiting van and taxi to take the Andrews to our temporary home in Colombo.

I wish I could accurately describe just five minutes of the drive from the airport into Colombo City. Perhaps it is the interesting psychological mix of jet lag, excitement, and exhaustion that produces a sort of overwhelming mental openness. It is as if the eyes have been propped open, and look at far too many things all at once, refusing to acknowledge the mind's insistent advice that perhaps enough has been taken in already.

Steve gave us an ongoing description of what we were driving past; the politics of the area and how they affected this group of people, or that particular housing project, but all I can really remember of that drive was cows in the trash, and people in the trash, and HORNS! Honking and honking and CARS breaking every possible traffic rule known anywhere: (lanes are only a guideline, you know; you can drive as many abreast as will fit—six cars across, all moving in various directions on a two-lane street, for example). I believe one of my first verbalized emotions in this country where I have come to make a positive contribution was an expletive, as several cars converged upon ours all at once going about forty miles per hour.

Within five days we were out of Colombo and touring the country with the Weirs. Our first trip was to Kandy—Buddhist center of the world and located in the center of Sri Lanka in the foothills. On our way, we stopped at the baby elephant orphanage. As Casey quickly found out, even baby elephants, four feet tall, are quite strong. The littlest fellow there was concerned that Casey might be in the way of his second bottle and "moved" her out of the way with his trunk, through the air and back next to Paula. Casey was delighted at the surprise ride.

We decided to make "adventure bracelets" and add a bead for each successful trip. Some trips were worth several beads, and sometimes a bead was earned simply by going to the post office!

Our car ride home from Kandy was a two-bead event. The rear wheel almost came off the van while swerving 'round and down the Kandy hills, and then the car overheated and came to a stop in a little village.

Our next trip was out to Hatton, high in the hills and tea estates. It is quite beautiful and much cooler than in Colombo. Sort of like Marquette in the early fall. There we met the Hatton committee for Habitat for Humanity and attended the first mortgage signing by homeowners. This took place in a tiny upstairs legal office that looked exactly like the one in *A Muppet's Christmas Carol.* The lawyer was anything but a "Scrooge," however, as he is very committed to Habitat's goals and is helping in any way he can.

Church was in a chapel on a hill with Reverend Kathiresapillai, a man who has devoted his life to serving others in this area of the world, and has been the main motivating source for Habitat in Hatton. Many of the tea pickers walked an hour or so to come to the service with their children. Everyone left their shoes at the door and sat on rough wooden planks. The hymn books were well worn, but everyone sang accompanied by Rajini Kathiresapillai. The entire service was in Tamil, but the message was in the faces and efforts of those present. We were humbled.

The trip home was on the INSIDE lane of the road down the mountains. We are thankful for small things!

—*Mark, Paula, Amelia, and Casey Andrews*
Sri Lanka

Others write about the climate and their dedicated national partners:

Cantel has two seasons—wet and dry. During the dry season we have warm, sunny days and cool mornings and evenings. The elevation is approximately 7,800 feet. During the months of December and January, it's possible to get frost in the mornings. Some nights it gets cold and we start "layering-up" with sweaters, bath robes, and coats to keep warm.

Our local committee and national partners have everything well organized. We are learning to stay out of the way when not needed and to pitch in and work when something needs to be done.

—*Ted and Louise Perry*
Guatemala

Sometimes they write about creative solutions to problems associated with launching a new Habitat affiliate:

> The tar paper over the thin walls is inadequate to keep out the wind or the bugs. The one window consists simply of a hole in the wall. Except for the light filtering through the walls, the house would be quite dark, even with the single bare bulb overhead. Water for cooking and cleaning is obtained from the spigot outside the front door. The bathroom, luxurious with its thin floor of rough troweled concrete, is shared with workers during the day. Six adults and two children call this thirty-square-meter (323-square-foot) shack their home. Welcome to the first Habitat house in Quimbaya!
>
> Perhaps we'd better explain. One prerequisite for a project like that in Quimbaya is a "bodega" to hold materials and tools during construction. Loss through theft or vandalism can be costly, but a night watchman can be costly as well. The committee's solution was to include a rough apartment in the design of the bodega which would allow one of the homeowner families to live rent-free while guarding the assets of the project by their constant presence.
>
> We initially objected. It's not "Habitatish" to move a family into a shack. But with brick covering the dirt floor, a good roof, a shower, and a flush toilet, this shack is better than many houses around Quimbaya. And the family is quite excited about the project and their role in lowering the costs.
>
> —*Grant and Sylvia Johnson*
> Colombia

And, the International Partners are amazed and delighted by the insights and perceptions of their children. John and Julia McCray-Goldsmith worked as International Partners for several years in Nicaragua before moving to Jamaica to help start the work there:

> Our children are healthy and growing and they delight us with their cultural insight and wisdom. Four-year-old Amos is sure that he lives in Kingston, Nicaragua, which is just down the street from his grandmother's house in America. The Global Village has become a reality in his mind!
>
> The Jamaican Habitat program has stabilized and matured. The first local affiliate, in inner-city Kingston, is building well. We have turned much of our attention to organizational development questions. We

plan to complete our (almost) seven-year commitment to Habitat for Humanity International this year, and hope to leave a strong board and well-established program in Jamaica.

—*John and Julia McCray-Goldsmith*
Jamaica

Sometimes they write about the response of the local people when Habitat's work finally begins to affect them:

In San Pedro Capula, the fifty homeowners will choose their house (probably through a raffle) and receive their house keys. The participants have been working incredibly hard. About half of them have already put in over two thousand hours, and they want this once-in-a-lifetime event to be a big hit. They will probably "fest" with a traditional Otami barbecue of about thirty to forty sheep. Not exciting for those who are vegetarians but a real treat for us carnivores.

In Dexthi Alberto, the folks are really "mellow," and they hardly batted an eye when I told them their project had been approved. They weren't able to keep their cool for long and big smiles soon broke out on all their usually stoic faces. They have already begun gathering rocks, sand, and the money for their down payments.

—*Eric Duell*
Mexico

Daniel Reyes is about fifty years old, and used to be a guerrilla fighter in the civil war of the 1980's but is now living a poor yet peaceful life as a farmer. He lives with his wife, seven children (ages eight through twenty-two), and his small cornfield behind the house. He is one of the fifteen regional committee members volunteering for Habitat, a very respectful, quiet man and a good friend of mine. The other day I visited him and his family and spent the night at their house. They have no water system (no toilets). They get water from a well across the road—using a rusty metal bucket on a rope. Food? There's enough but it is almost always the same: beans, rice, eggs, corn, corn tortillas (and vegetables and chicken several times a week). To go to town, they walk forty-five minutes on the dirt road to catch a bus on the main road (then a forty-five-minute bus ride). The family has very few possessions: basic furniture, clothes, and a few small personal things. Their house is OK; it has electricity and is large enough for the nine of them—which is unusual here. However, the house is made of adobe (dirt) bricks, has dirt floors, and only one door in the front. With open doorways in the back, they have no way to lock the house . . . and the chickens and dogs live in the house with them. (This is the typical kind of family we are working with here.)

When the Habitat program began here, Señor Reyes volunteered to serve on the regional committee, and he applied to have a Habitat house. But when he started working on the 'family selection' subcommittee, he began visiting families living in very bad conditions (houses of bamboo, for example). He then took his Habitat application form out of the file and tore it into pieces, saying, "I don't really NEED a new house and I do not want to take a house from someone who has greater needs than me."

—*Dane Fountain*
El Salvador

At other times, the International Partners write about the impact their work has on visitors and work campers.

The Nogales Habitat for Humanity affiliate is located on the Arizona/Mexico border about sixty miles south of Tucson. With the close proximity to the United States, this project has the advantage to receive many visitors and work groups from the U.S. The area where the project is located is very hilly with poor roads and limited city services. It is quite a contrast to any American city or town.

One youth group from a Tucson church arrived at Nogales Habitat to spend a Saturday working with the Mexican people. After a long day of hard work, carrying concrete blocks up a steep hill to the location where the Habitat house was being built, four of the youth returned to our house. As they rested and reflected on the day, one young teen looked at her hands and found several scratches on them. Her friend asked her, "Why did you give that girl your gloves?"

"I wanted to," she replied.

"But, you really shouldn't have. Look at your hands."

"I wanted to!" she insisted. "That girl has to go home to a

crummy old shack and I have a nice home to return to with medicine and comforts."

The young girl shared further with us that she would at times
complain about things she didn't have, but after coming to Nogales
she could see that her wants and needs would be seen in a different
perspective.

—Paul and Janet Burger
Mexico

Often International Partners write us after they return, their words
full of how truly overwhelming it is to be involved in Habitat's overseas
work. The sentiments of two such people people provide a fitting ending
to this chapter:

It is said that once you have lived overseas, you will never be the same
again. That is true for us. We can't go to [the grocery store] and not
be reminded of our hungry neighbors. We can't visit the malls and
not see the rags the children wear every day. God has changed us.
There is a huge chasm that separates us from those in need. [We're
reminded] of the time Bill Moyers interviewed Southern activist
Miles Horton. At the end of the interview, Bill asked Miles what the
big issue would be for the [future]. Miles thoughtfully responded
that the crisis between the haves and have-nots would be the big
issue and that it would be very painful because we all have family and
friends on both sides. . . .

—Mark and Margee Frey
Former International Partners in Kinshasha, Zaire

Prospective Habitat homeowners at a site where homes are being built with disabled persons in Ethiopia.

CHAPTER NINE

Who Did You Say Was Sponsoring That House?

The New Corporate Partnerships

THERE'S A SECRET about corporate America. It's made up of people who live in houses, have families, go to churches, and who know that being in business means not only producing goods and services but also helping neighbors—especially those in greatest need.

Many corporate leaders have discovered the thrill of helping their neighbors by swinging hammers to build simple, decent places to live. Within the last five years, they have discovered Habitat for Humanity and the response has been amazing, providing a tremendous boost to the work of Habitat throughout the United States and Canada and in other countries.

Some sponsor houses, others donate materials, some have made interesting commitments ranging from building a Habitat house for every new store opened to matching grants to using a Habitat blitz build as an incentive program for their agents. Corporate thinking is creative, to say the least—and again, the result is a win/win proposition in every way. Companies help by donating money and materials of all kinds, from light fixtures to doors to caulking to paint to cement mixers to tools. And, corporations often make available highly-skilled people such as architects, heavy-equipment operators, managers, and building supervisors.

Habitat for Humanity benefits tremendously from these multi-faceted expressions of partnership with various corporations. But the companies benefit too. They have the joyous satisfaction of participating in an activity that is uplifting to the community, and it casts the company in a very favorable light. Furthermore, working together to build a house also builds strong relationships among company personnel. Many corporate leaders have told me how much this aspect of the work means to them.

Our first corporate partner was BellSouth Telecommunications.

Since 1990, this partnership has been responsible for more than seventy Habitat houses, and the building continues. BellSouth teams, made up of BellSouth employees from nine Southern states, build the houses. In fact, BellSouth Telecommunications challenged itself to have a corporate team in each of the nine states of its service region by the end of 1994. I might add that BellSouth accomplished that goal.

The partnership works like this: The company provides a quarter of the cost of each house, their local employees raise another quarter and recruit volunteers to build it, then the local Habitat affiliate raises the remainder of the cost. This fine company has been a pioneer with Habitat—and a faithful one—and that's what makes the company so special to Habitat.

Another very exciting partnership is with America's Favorite Chicken, which owns Popeye's Famous Fried Chicken and Biscuits, and Churchs Chicken. Chief Executive Officer Frank Belatti contacted us expressing a deep concern for the people who lived in the communities serviced by his stores and offered to fully sponsor one hundred Habitat homes to be built over a five-year period—an ultimate commitment of three-and-a-half million dollars. He doubled his commitment a year later. Since then, he has set up a program within his company called "Dream Builders," which has already built houses all over the United States. The company also plans to build Habitat houses in Jamaica and other countries where they have stores. Frank believes in the Habitat dream—that everyone deserves to have a simple, decent place to live. And he believes the relationship will be good for his company, good for Habitat, good for the communities, and certainly good for the thousand or so people who will live in the two hundred houses built by America's Favorite Chicken. Frank and his wife Cathy also have had a very personal interest in

The employees of BellSouth Telecommunications at work on the BellSouth house during the 20/20,000 Blitz Build in Americus in April 1993.

Habitat. Their daughter Alyson served as a Habitat volunteer in Ghana, West Africa in 1995.

One of the most comprehensive corporate partnerships is with Target Stores. The name of that partnership says it all when it comes to the kind of hope corporate partnerships are making possible: "Building a Wonderful Life."

Beginning in 1993, Target has been building a Habitat house in every community in which it has built a new store. In 1994, forty houses were built and the company projects that they will have completed one hundred Habitat houses by the end of 1995.

Singer Amy Grant, spokesperson for Target, promoted the Habitat for Humanity partnership on her nationwide tour in early 1995.

Typical of a Target-sponsored Habitat house was one built with the Ayala family in partnership with San Bernadino, California Habitat for Humanity. More than six hundred Target employees joined other Habitat volunteers to build the house. Doreen Hicks, an employee of the Fontana Target Store, summed up feelings about the project: "You go home stinky and dirty, but you feel so good inside."

(Photo by Kimberly Prenda)

Millard Fuller joins singer Amy Grant at the dedication of a new Habitat house in Nashville, Tennessee, sponsored by Target.

Some corporations by their very names are perfect Habitat partners. The Home Depot, HunterDouglas Window Fashions, Sterling Plumbing Group, Centex Homes, Ryland Home and Mortgage Company, John Wieland Homes, Milwaukee Electric Tool Corporation, and Larson Manufacturing Company are companies that have made quite a difference in our ability to build and build cheaply, yet with attention to quality.

For instance, Larson Manufacturing Company headquartered in Brookings, South Dakota and the nation's leading storm/screen door manufacturer, is now donating their high-quality doors to local affiliates across the United States in all areas that the company services and is even delivering the doors at no cost. They contributed product worth more than four hundred thousand dollars in 1994, in addition to multiple-house sponsorships at special Habitat events like the Jimmy Carter Work Project. At the 1994 Jimmy Carter Work Project in Eagle Butte, South Dakota, Larson Manufacturing sponsored one-and-a-half homes—in addition to making a sizeable material donation. President Dale Larson and his wife Pat were among the company volunteers who helped build the houses they sponsored. Larson employee Mary Ann Holler, one of those company volunteers, said, "It was one of the most positive experiences of my life, and I know that most every other Larson employee who was there feels the same."

HunterDouglas Window Fashions provides all the custom window dressings for Habitat houses built in the United States. Orders are taken through our Gifts-In-Kind Department at Habitat headquarters in Americus, then shipped directly from HunterDouglas manufacturing plants to Habitat affiliates.

Centex Corporation is the nation's largest residential builder and has operations in mortgage banking, contracting and construction services, construction products, and savings and loan. Between 1991 and 1994, Centex built approximately sixty-five houses with Habitat for Humanity affiliates in the United States and in 1995 signed a contract with Habitat for Humanity International that will provide funding and volunteer partnerships through the year 2000.

Yet another corporate partner providing significant product to Habitat for Humanity is the Dow Chemical Company, headquartered in Midland, Michigan. Dow has been the exclusive provider of rigid foam insulation to U.S. Habitat affiliates for 1994 and 1995—a contribution valued at a quarter of a million dollars each year. The company also has sponsored houses at Jimmy Carter Work Projects. Kathleen Bader, vice president of Dow's Fabricated Products Division, had this to say about the partnership:

> "Habitat for Humanity is a program that has a lot of heart, rings a bell with our people, and fits in with the Dow Corporate culture. This is a commitment from our hearts, not just our pocketbooks. We really see what can happen when people give time and energy to help someone else realize the dream of homeownership."

The Darworth Company, headquartered in Simsbury, Connecticut, manufactures caulk sealant. They have provided all interior and exterior caulking for Habitat houses in the United States!

The Home Depot has worked with hundreds of local Habitat affiliates. The company built sixty-three houses in 1994 with Habitat affiliates, based on store-to-affiliate grassroots relationships. Additionally, multiple Home Depot stores have extended lines of credit to local Habitat affiliates. The company has committed to building eight houses for the "One Hundred Homes: Building an Atlanta Legacy" project in 1995–96. The company also sponsored and built an environmentally friendly "green" house at the 30/30,000 Blitz Build in Americus in June 1994, and has discussed the possibility of duplicating the project in other locations.

One of our newest corporate partners is the Sterling Plumbing Group, a division of Kohler Plumbing, located outside Chicago. An exclusive agreement was signed with them for plumbing fixtures amounting to a quarter of a million dollars. This partnership was announced at the National Association of Home Builders Convention in Houston, Texas in January 1995.

Speaking of the National Association of Home Builders, while they are an association and not a business corporation, they certainly are wonderful partners with Habitat for Humanity. The association consists of more than eight hundred state and local builders' associations representing 160,000 members in the United States. The association entered into partnership with Habitat for Humanity International in 1992. That year they matched local associations with local Habitat affiliates to build houses across the country in a program called "Homes Across America." Hundreds of local builders' associations assist Habitat affiliates in countless ways. This extensive partnership is invaluable to Habitat for Humanity.

Another association that provides millions of dollars and thousands of volunteers to Habitat for Humanity is the National Fraternal Congress. The NFC is an umbrella organization for a hundred fraternal insurance societies such as Woodmen of the World, Aid Association For Lutherans, Lutheran Brotherhood, National Catholic Life, Mennonite Mutual Aid, Knights of Columbus, and Sons of Norway. They have a combined membership of ten million people. Habitat for Humanity was adopted as the national cause of the NFC in 1990.

Our partnership with General Motors Acceptance Corporation's Residential Funding Corporation (RFC) is truly unique. One of RFC's executives approached Twin Cities (Minneapolis/St. Paul, Minnesota) Habitat for Humanity director Steve Seidel and asked, "Is there a way we can leverage the properties you've already developed?" The response was the creation of the "Homes First: Sharing the Dream" program by the company that provides long-term, no-interest or low-interest loans to Habitat affiliates. The loans are secured by liens that Habitat holds on the houses it has sold and financed. What's the benefit? Capital is freed for the affiliates to enable them to build more houses faster. Best of all, the plan in no way affects our no-interest program with our homeowners.

Our Corporate Sponsorship Program has simple aims for company partners:

- Provide materials to Habitat for Humanity
- Encourage employee volunteer activities with local affiliates
- Provide financial support to local affiliates
- Raise the level of awareness about the work of Habitat for Humanity
- Underscore company commitment to communities they serve

- Participate in and support special events, such as blitz builds, sponsored by Habitat for Humanity International.[1]

The 1994 Jimmy Carter Work Project in Eagle Butte, South Dakota was a study in corporate generosity. Many companies donated hundreds of thousands of dollars in cash and products to sponsor houses there. They also discovered that partnering with Habitat yields personal returns as well.

John Shawhan, Marketing Systems director for Indianapolis Life Insurance, says his company always is looking for better ways to team build. "We've offered different incentives over the years. We've sent people to resorts. But we find it's more productive for the company if we offer something like the Jimmy Carter Work Project. So 1994's incentive was 'a trip to a mystery destination with the CEO for an experience you've never had before.'"

Joe Urso from Madison, Wisconsin, one of the seven winning field agents, was more than a bit surprised when told the destination of his "mystery trip." "We're going to *where* and do *what?*" was his first response. Later, he said, "It was really hard work, but I want to do it again. Now when people ask me about where I've gone when I've won incentives, I can tell them: Bermuda, Hawaii, Quebec, and Eagle Butte."[1]

Richard Manoogian, chairman and CEO of the MASCO Corporation, a Fortune 500 building products conglomerate, brought his personal collection of Western art to Sioux Falls, South Dakota to display for a fund-raiser which helped kick off the Jimmy Carter Work Project at Eagle Butte. Money raised at the art show was used at the Jimmy Carter Work Project and at the local affiliate in Sioux Falls.

The corporate partnership program has been so successful, with new partners coming on board all the time, that it is impossible to list everyone. However, I would like to mention a few more corporate partners, because they are so significant to this growing house-building venture. Each one creates new excitement. All sorts of companies are figuring out ways to help Habitat's cause. From local businesses to huge corporations, they are building houses across the country, giving what they have through funding, volunteering, and donating materials.

San Francisco-based PMI Mortgage Insurance Company began their partnership with Habitat for Humanity in 1993. PMI supports Habitat with corporate contributions, grants to local Habitat affiliates, and volunteer work projects in cities where the company does business.

United Consumers Club continues to raise funds in its franchise cities, so far helping seventy different local Habitat affiliates. Nearly a quarter of a million dollars was distributed to those affiliates in 1994.

Coldwell Banker, headquartered in Mission Viejo, California, also made Habitat for Humanity its official philanthropic partner in 1994. Many of the company's local offices throughout the country actively help their local Habitat affiliates with funding and volunteers.

One of our most generous corporate partners is The Thompson's Company, a leading manufacturer and marketer of quality home care and do-it-yourself products. The company has sponsored several blitz build houses and they also supply water-proofing and paint products for Habitat affiliates across the country.

Maxwell House Coffee joined the Habitat for Humanity sponsor list in January 1995 with a kick-off promotion pledging a percentage of its coffee sales during the first week of the new year. The company also plans to build houses in areas where they have packaging and distribution facilities.

Another very new partnership program is with MBNA America. Habitat for Humanity International has entered into a three-year royalty arrangement with MBNA America to issue a VISA credit card featuring the Habitat for Humanity International name and logo. The program will benefit Habitat by increasing public awareness and by providing royalties for each credit card issued and for a portion of each transaction charged by cardholders. The marketing campaign was launched in February 1995.

MBNA America, incidentally, has been a corporate supporter of Habitat for Humanity since 1990. They have sponsored houses and contributed generously to our new Habitat headquarters in Americus.

Local business partnerships see a difference right around the corner in the help they give. Sometimes local companies help best by encouraging their employees to take part. Corporex Company of Covington, Kentucky did just that in asking Jim Mouhourits and other employees to help build Habitat houses in the local area. Interviewed by the *Cincinnati Enquirer,* Mouhourits said that he and fellow volunteers have been able to make a "little bit of difference in somebody's life. We get to meet these families and they become special to us."

American Investors, a Topeka business, decided to build a house and encouraged their employees to help any way they could. The employees raised ten thousand dollars by holding a huge garage sale. The parent company matched that amount in order to blitz build their Habitat house. "Everyone was a little more sore on Monday than they're used to," said Mark Heitz, chairman of the company," but they saw the end result of their work, got to know each other as well as knowing the Habitat partner family while working together. There's just no downside from our perspective," he told the *Topeka Capital-Journal.*

Banks are finding that partnership with Habitat for Humanity is beneficial in many ways. Commerce Bank and Trust in Topeka is one such bank. Executive assistant Mary Borland told a *Topeka Capital-Journal* reporter that Commerce Bank decided to work with Habitat because almost all the money and time donated to Habitat went directly to building the homes. But as the employees began raising money and working together, they benefited in a surprising way.

"It really improved our staff communications," Mary Borland said. "You end up working side by side with the senior vice president or a member of the board of directors." The bank donated thirty thousand dollars needed to build the house, then the employees used contacts to acquire discounts on materials.

Banks also are helping in Canada. Royal Bank of Canada and The Canadian Imperial Bank of Commerce have contributed annually to Habitat for Humanity of Canada, and the Canadian Imperial Bank has encouraged all its branches to accept donations from customers to Habitat. Many other corporate partners in Canada are helping the work in that country to grow dramatically.

Meanwhile, back in the United States the Federal Home Loan Bank of Cincinnati gave twenty-five thousand dollars to Covington, Kentucky Habitat for Humanity. Other local banks kicked in an additional thirty thousand dollars. Federal Home Loan Bank president Charles Thiemann told the *Cincinnati Enquirer* that his bank was committed to our vision of helping people build and own simple, decent places to live because the "family is the bedrock of society, and housing is a basic need."

The gifts were part of the "Kentucky Homecoming '94" campaign to build one hundred and one houses all across the state in the summer of 1994. Elizabeth Lloyd (Libby) Jones, wife of Kentucky Governor Brereton Jones, served as honorary chairperson of the campaign.

It was a success in large part because of the extensive involvement and support of various corporate partners such as the Federal Home Loan Bank, Community Bankers of Kentucky, Cellular One, and many others.

All across the country, the Federal Home Loan Bank Board is helping Habitat for Humanity. Regina Nobles, director of community investment for Habitat for Humanity, estimates that by mid-April 1995 more than fifteen million dollars had been provided by the FHLB to hundreds of Habitat affiliates through the Affordable Housing Program to member banks, who then pass the funds on to Habitat affiliates. This FHLB/Habitat partnership has helped to house approximately 2,400 families across the country.

Member banks also provide volunteer work crews and help with family recruitment and financial training.

As these examples demonstrate, corporate partners are increasingly significant in the growing success of Habitat for Humanity all across North America, and I am convinced that these partnerships will be ever more significant in our nationwide and worldwide work in the years ahead. I am profoundly grateful for the concerned men and women who lead these fine companies and who are so generous to the expanding work of Habitat for Humanity. In partnership, we are making a difference—and that difference gets bigger all the time as we continue to work together.

CHAPTER TEN

You Want to Do *What* by *When?*

No Shacks by the Year 2000—The Sumter County Initiative: Why Others Can Dream the Same Dream

A DYNAMIC HABITAT for Humanity program in a community brings a special dimension into town. It allows people to see how concerted action makes a difference. Neighborhoods are transformed, and people who have been part of a city's problem become part of its solution.

So why wouldn't every community dream of transforming all the neighborhoods in need of hope and change?

Is getting rid of all substandard housing in a whole community, a city, state, or even a nation just an impossible dream?

I don't think so.

While most nations of the world have poverty housing and homelessness, some nations—primarily in Western Europe—do not. Likewise, in the United States, while a great many towns and cities have slum neighborhoods and homeless people, there are communities that do not.

Hence, we know from simply observing the actual situation in our country and in the world that what is being proposed is possible. It's already been done in some places! We can eliminate poverty housing and homelessness, *everywhere*. It only takes a commitment of the will, a total determination to tackle the problem and conquer it. And, of course, constantly seeking the guidance of God. That is so important because, as the Bible says, it is only *with God* that all things are possible.

Lately, I have been talking up the idea that poverty housing *really* can be eliminated. However, I want to prod communities, towns, and cities not to work to eliminate poverty housing and homelessness in some distant future. I issue the challenge to begin thinking about a *certain date* by which substandard housing and homelessness will be eliminated in their local areas.

I know the power of "large plans." I know big things can happen from saying seemingly impossible ideas out loud.

In September 1994, I was keynote speaker when the Dallas Citizens Council and the Dallas Coalition for Affordable Housing launched a program to build thirty thousand new houses over the coming decade in the city of Dallas, Texas. Habitat for Humanity will help build a portion of those houses, working hand-in-glove with these two groups. That is the kind of thing we want to promote—bold, cooperative programs. Let's build thirty thousand houses in ten years, they said—and they will do it. Two bankers stood up during the meeting and pledged one million dollars each to the project.

We want leaders as well as ordinary people in a community to be ashamed to have visitors come to their town and find that there are people living like rats over in the bad sections of town.

That's how I feel.

I want you to reflect on something. The word *grace* is full of powerful meaning. We talk about the "grace of God." In common speech we often remark, or hear someone say, "Only by the grace of God," was I not injured, or did not get sick, or whatever. Another common expression is, "Saved by the grace of God. . . ."

With grace, there is always the element of our being undeserving. "While we were yet sinners Christ died for us." Such phrases help us to understand that God's love extends to everyone with literally nobody left out. Even though we are undeserving, God still loves us.

One of the best known and most loved hymns in our culture is "Amazing Grace." Listen to the words of that great hymn:

"Amazing grace, how sweet the sound
That saved a wretch like me.
I once was lost, but now I'm found,
Was blind, but now I see."

John Newton, a former slave trader, knew of his own unworthiness but he had assurance of God's love. Newton wrote down his concept of grace as he knew it, and the result was "Amazing Grace." God gave to him, as He gives to everyone, His matchless grace. God's love—His wonderful grace—extends even to the most undeserving person. That being the case, we should always extend our love to others around us, even as God does—to the least, to the unloved, to those left behind and left out.

Grace is about *giving,* and giving in an open-handed way, without regard to the *quid pro quo.* Grace gives. Grace is concerned. Grace is full of love and kindness and all goodness. Grace is full of love, kindness, and goodness because grace is full of God—and God is full of grace.

A graceful person is not only one who is beautiful, walks in a nice flowing way, and speaks in soothing tones. A truly graceful person is one whose life is characterized by being outward oriented and concerned about the well-being of others.

Likewise, a community which is graceful is one where people are concerned about one another. Walls are down both in the mind and on the ground. Instead, bridges have been constructed. A graceful town is one with no dark corners and no forgotten people. All are loved and cared for. Love is the ethic of such a place.

Since people are so graceful in the town, they would be appalled and deeply ashamed to know that someone in their midst was living in slum housing—or worse still, out of doors. Allowing such would be unthinkable.

Our mandate in Habitat for Humanity is to work diligently to help bring into being graceful communities, towns, and cities. This is so important because the alternative is *disgraceful.* You see, the opposite of grace is *disgrace.*

We must begin to think like this. If we do, we will increasingly see transformations in our communities. We truly must be ashamed—both as individuals and as whole towns, and cities and ultimately as nations and the world—to realize that fellow citizens, brother and sister human beings, are living in miserable conditions. Loving our neighbors as we love ourselves

(Photo by Julie Lopez)

Poor families often spend 60 percent or more of their income for inadequate housing.

must become real. We must know our neighbors' names, their addresses, and their needs. We must act responsibly to meet those needs. For Habitat for Humanity, it means identifying where all the people are who live in bad housing, then work diligently and systematically—and with real urgency—to get them into good, graceful places to live.

The more I thought about this whole subject, the more I became convinced that we should model this idea somewhere. Where would be more logical than the hometown headquarters of Habitat for Humanity International—Americus, Georgia and surrounding Sumter County?

This small town and county in southwest Georgia have a stable population of about twenty-seven thousand people. When we built that first house for Bo and Emma Johnson at Koinonia Farm in 1969, nearly half our citizens lived in substandard housing. Over the years Koinonia—and later Habitat for Humanity—built hundreds of houses. Even so, several hundred families still lived in poverty housing. In short, the situation remained disgraceful.

Actually, from the moment we began to build houses, I have dreamed of completely eliminating poverty housing in our own backyard. By 1985, the worldwide work of Habitat for Humanity had grown so dramatically that we had to build a new headquarters that took up a city block. The area around our new headquarters had been a sea of shacks, but they now were gone, replaced with fifty new Habitat houses. By 1992, nearly three hundred homes had been built in the county by Koinonia and Habitat for Humanity.

But many shacks remained. I made a quick study, and estimated that we needed to build or renovate about five hundred more houses in Americus and Sumter County to completely eliminate substandard housing.

At our current rate of building five houses a year locally, the job would take a hundred years to finish. I wanted to see poverty housing eliminated in our home area in my lifetime, and as healthy as I might be, I probably wasn't going to live that long!

I decided to be bold with a logical extension of Habitat's "crazy idea that works." When the international board of directors met in January 1992, I proposed an initiative to eliminate poverty housing in our town and county by the end of the decade.

The proposal initially met with resistance, but eventually the board enthusiastically accepted and embraced the idea. I believed a daring initiative like this would have an energizing effect on the whole ministry—a beacon of light, an example of what was possible in other places.

If we could do it in Americus and Sumter County, then anyone could do it—anywhere.

To actually eliminate poverty housing in a specific part of the country would be a powerful demonstration of the effectiveness of the theology of the hammer. In fact, it was only appropriate for Habitat to eliminate substandard housing in our own hometown and county as quickly as possible, since that's what we were advocating that others do elsewhere. That was my argument.

Of course, I knew we couldn't do the entire job on our own. The whole community would have to embrace the idea. I knew we could only be the catalyst—that an umbrella organization would need to be formed to bring in churches, the Housing Authority, civic clubs and other organizations, mobilizing everyone to make this happen. It was decided that the name for this umbrella group would be the Sumter County Initiative. I had a firm conviction that people in our area would rally behind this idea. Times had changed. I really believed this bold idea would work. I had already gotten numerous letters of support to offer the board from community leaders—letters such as these:

> I very much support your proposed recommendation that we eliminate all sub-standard housing in the City of Americus and Sumter County by the end of the decade. This is an enormous goal, but with all the available resources we have working together, I believe it's a goal we can surely reach.
>
> *—John Linneman*
> Community Development Director

> The Sumter County Board of Commissioners pledge to you our 100 percent support and are committed to helping in every way that we possibly can.
>
> *—J. Wade Halstead*
> Chairman

> On behalf of the City Council, I am pleased to write this letter supporting Habitat's initiative to eliminate poverty housing in Americus and Sumter County by the year 2000. This will not only provide better housing for our citizens but will also enhance Sumter County's image to the world as a community that cares about its people. We wholeheartedly stand behind your efforts, and if you need anything else from the City, please do not hesitate to contact me.
>
> *—Tom Gailey*
> Mayor

Even Jimmy Carter wrote an enthusiastic letter of endorsement and support:

> I think this is a worthy goal and one which can be reached. I also believe it is an endeavor which will elicit a very positive response from people both within Americus and Sumter County and throughout the country. Your idea that the town and county of Habitat headquarters should be free of poverty housing is sound and exciting.

Our 20/20,000th Blitz Build, where we'd build twenty houses and the twentieth house would be Habitat's 20,000th house built, was planned right here in Americus in 1993 to start everything.

But could one small community come up with enough sponsors to build that many houses?

You bet.

Sponsors began to pour in as the community responded in a study of how big dreams can be fulfilled locally—together. Each house would cost twenty thousand dollars. Citizens Bank of Americus agreed to build the milestone 20,000th house. First United Methodist Church committed to building a house. First Presbyterian and Bethesda Baptist formed a partnership to build a house together, as did Allen Chapel African Methodist Episcopal and Calvary Episcopal. Koinonia committed to supervising the building of a memorial house for a beloved Habitat staff member who had died, and the funds came rolling in. The National Association of Home Builders built in memory of one of their beloved young staffers. It was co-sponsored by Meredith Corporation and Chevy Trucks. The Tog Shop, an outstanding local industry, the John S. and James L. Knight Foundation, Weyerhauser Company, the United Methodist Committee on Relief, BellSouth Telecommunications, Inc., Georgia Power Company, and Deloitte and Touche—all with local ties, sponsored homes. The remaining houses were sponsored by various other organizations.

It *does* work. It *is* working.

So we blitz-built the twenty houses during Holy Week. All of the houses were completed on Good Friday. The families moved in on Saturday and woke up for the first time in their new homes on Easter Sunday morning. It was glorious! We even had an Easter sunrise service at the site. My son Chris preached and, as you can imagine, it was the most meaningful Easter service of my life.

In 1994 we did it again. Our 30/30,000 project, an encore of the 20/20,000 project, went off without a hitch. When the thirtieth house was finished, we also had finished thirty thousand houses worldwide. Here in our small town, we'd already done fifty houses within the span of two years just in the two blitz builds, and dozens more also had gone up. Plus, other groups were erecting or renovating several more. We now estimate that until the end of the decade, Habitat, the City of Americus, and other organizations such as Christian Rebuilders will build or renovate sixty to eighty houses a year.

We *can* do it. We *will*.

As poverty housing is being eliminated right here in Habitat headquarters' own backyard by the year 2000, so is it in the Yure River Basin in northern Honduras. Through Habitat's tithing program, the international affiliate has been linked to the Sumter County Initiative, so all poverty housing is going to be done away with there during the same time.

We set a date—a realistic date.

Others can too. When I was in Sarasota, Florida in March 1995, I learned to my delight that they are beginning to talk about a date for eliminating all substandard housing in that Florida city.

What date could you realistically think about for eliminating poverty housing in your own town, ensuring everybody a simple, decent place to live?

I often say that there is a difference between faith and foolishness. We want to challenge people to get as close to foolishness as they can . . . without crossing the line. Think creatively and boldly! Go ahead and set a date! You can do it! With God, all things are possible!

(Photo by Julie Lopez)

SCI board members break ground at the 30/30,000 Blitz Build site in Americus, Georgia.

As we get closer and closer to seeing our town and county's plan for eliminating every last shack and getting the people into good houses, I know there will be more communities to accept the challenge. Seeing is believing.

I invite you to come see our dream coming true in Americus and Sumter County. Pick up a hammer and be a part.

And what about Habitat's far-flung goal? What about eliminating substandard housing and homelessness from the face of the earth?

I want to build houses for a million people—just as we have dreamed of doing for many years—and go on from there.

I can see the changes that ridding my own hometown and county of all but the last of the shacks has created. You have seen—or read about—the changes caused by ridding your own community and others of substandard housing. Spirits are lifted. Crime is reduced. Love abounds. Faith is restored—faith in each other and in God.

We may not see it in our lifetimes, but why can't our children see it? Or does the problem seem too big?

It *is* big, I agree.

I was thinking the other day about the Los Angeles riots of 1992. After the riots, Habitat for Humanity launched a campaign to raise special matching funds to build homes in Los Angeles and other riot-stricken cities. Since then, scores of homes have been completed in Southern California, and plans are in place for many more.

What impact could Habitat for Humanity realistically have on a place with such a large problem?

My answer is this: I liken it to the biblical image of leaven. By itself, leaven does nothing: Put just a small amount into dough and it will make the whole thing rise. Every house we build makes a unique statement. We want to make providing basic shelter a matter of conscience. We want it to be socially, morally, politically, and religiously unacceptable to allow substandard housing and homelessness. We're more than a construction company. What makes Habitat work is the spiritual motivation behind it. And that spiritual motivation knows one small truth beyond the large fact of poverty housing in our world.

Everyone—all of us, every last person on God's earth—deserves decent shelter. It speaks to the most basic of human needs—our home—

the soil from which all of us, every last person, either blossoms or withers. We each have need of food, clothing, education, medical care, and companionship; but first, we must have a place to live and grow. Most of us take our own homes for granted, but no Habitat homeowner or volunteer ever does.

Here, then, is the idea to set loose in the land: *Everyone should have a simple, decent place to live.*

We have the know-how in the world to house everyone. We have the resources in the world to house everyone. All that's missing is the *will* to do it.

Make no small plans.

Can we build houses for a million people? Why not? Why not a million houses for five million people? Why not even more?

Affiliate Covenant

*A Basic Covenant Between Habitat for Humanity
International and an Approved Habitat
Affiliate Project*

Preface

Habitat for Humanity International and the Habitat for Humanity affiliate work as partners in this ecumenical Christian housing ministry. The affiliate works with donors, volunteers and homeowners to create decent, affordable housing for those in need, and to make shelter a matter of conscience with people everywhere. Although Habitat for Humanity International will assist with information resources, training, publications, prayer support and in other ways, the affiliate is primarily and directly responsible for the legal, organizational, fund-raising, family selection and nurture, financial and construction aspects of the work.

Mission Statement

Habitat for Humanity works in partnership with God and people everywhere, from all walks of life, to develop communities with God's people in need by building and renovating houses, so that there are decent houses in decent communities in which God's people can live and grow into all that God intended.

Method of Operation

Habitat for Humanity sponsors projects in habitat development by constructing modest but adequate housing. Habitat also seeks to associate with other organizations functioning with purposes consistent with those of Habitat for Humanity International and the affiliate, as stated in the Articles of Incorporation of both Habitat organizations.

Foundational Principles

1. Habitat for Humanity seeks to demonstrate the love and teachings of Jesus Christ to all people. While Habitat is a Christian organization, it invites and welcomes affiliate board members, volunteers and donors from other faiths actively committed to Habitat's Mission, Method of Operation, and Principles. The board will reflect the ethnic diversity of the area to be served.

2. Habitat for Humanity is a people-to-people partnership drawing families and communities in need together with volunteers and resources to build decent, affordable housing for needy people. Habitat is committed to the development and uplifting of families and communities, not only to the construction of houses.

3. Habitat for Humanity builds, renovates, and repairs simple, decent and affordable housing with people who are living in inadequate housing and who are unable to secure adequate housing by conventional means.

4 Habitat for Humanity selects homeowner families according to criteria that do not discriminate on the basis of race, creed, or ethnic background. All homeowners contribute "sweat equity;" they work as partners with the affiliate and other volunteers to accomplish Habitat's mission, both locally and worldwide.

5. Habitat for Humanity sells houses to selected families with no profit or interest added. House payments will be used for the construction or renovation of additional affordable housing.

6. Habitat for Humanity is a global partnership. In recognition of and commitment to that global partnership, each affiliate is expected to contribute at least 10 percent of its cash contributions to Habitat's international work. Funds specifically designated by a donor for local work only may be excluded from the tithe.

7. Habitat for Humanity does not seek and will not accept government funds for the construction of houses. Habitat for Humanity welcomes partnership with governments that includes accepting funds to help set the stage for the construction of houses, provided it does not limit our ability to proclaim our Christian witness, and further provided that affiliates do not

become dependent on or controlled by government funds thus obtained. Setting the stage is interpreted to include land, houses for rehabilitation, infrastructure for streets, utilities, and administrative expenses. Funding from third parties who accept government funds with sole discretion over their use shall not be considered as government funds for Habitat purposes.

Agreement to Covenant

In affirmation of the Mission, Method of Operation and Principles stated in this Covenant, we,_____, a Habitat for Humanity affiliate, covenant with other affiliates and Habitat for Humanity International to accomplish our mission. Each partner commits to enhancing that ability to carry out this mission by: supporting effective communication among affiliates, Habitat for Humanity International and regional offices; sharing annual reports; participating in regional and national training events; and participating in a biennial review and planning session between each affiliate and the regional office.

This Covenant is valid upon approval by each member of the affiliate board of directors and a designated representative of Habitat for Humanity International.

For further information about Habitat for Humanity International, write or call the Regional or National Center nearest you (see list in Appendix Two) or the International headquarters:

Habitat for Humanity International
121 Habitat Street
Americus, GA 31709-3498
Telephone: (912) 924-6935
FAX: (912) 924-6541

International, National, and Regional Centers

INTERNATIONAL

Karen Foreman, Director, International Affiliates
121 Habitat Street
Americus, GA 31709-3498
(912) 924-6935
f: (912) 924-0577

AFRICA/MIDDLE EAST

Botswana National Office
c/o Thapelong Catholic Mission
P. O. Box 285
Kanye
Botswana
a: (011) 267-341-513
f: (011) 267-340-147

Burundi National Office
Contact: Habitat for Humanity
International
Americus, GA 31709-3498
(912) 924-6935, ext. 226/228

**Central African Republic
National Office**
B. P. 862
Bangui
Central African Republic
a: (011)236-61-77-26
f: (011)236-61-61-36

Habitat for Humanity Egypt
Habitat for Humanity
c/o CEOSS—El Motomadia
Nabil Samuel
P. O. Box 1304
11511 Cairo
Egypt
a: (011) 202-906-683
f: (011) 202-904-995

Habitat for Humanity—Port Said
Bishop Tadros
c/o DDSA
P. O. Box 5995
W. Heliopolis
Egypt
Phone/Fax: (011) 20-66-238-668

Ethiopia National Office
P. O. Box 8953
Addis Ababa
Ethiopia
a: (011) 251-1-186749
f: (011) 251-1-610063

Ghana National Office
P. O. Box C-81
Cantonment
Accra
Ghana
Phone/Fax: (011) 233-21-231-268

Kenya National Office
P. O. Box 17945
Nairobi
Kenya
a: (011) 254-2-745-854
f: (011) 254-2-560-374

Malawi National Office
Mpingwe Avenue
P. O. Box 5848
Limbe
Malawi
a: (011) 265-640073/640763
f: (011) 265-640-910

South Africa National Office
P. O. Box 61142
Marshalltown 2107
South Africa
a: (011) 2711-836-0710
f: (011) 2711-836-0711

Nigeria
Contact: Habitat for Humanity
International
Americus, GA 31709-3498
(912) 924-6935

Tanzania National Office
P. O. Box 4148
Dodoma
Tanzania
Phone/Fax: (011) 255-61-24738

Uganda National Office
P. O. Box 9873
Kampala
Uganda
Phone/Fax: (011) 256-41-241-835

Zaire National Office
Habitat Pou l'Humanite
CBZO B. P. 4728
Kinshasa II
Zaire
a: (011) 243-12-50792
f: 1-212-376-9396

Zambia Habitat for Humanity
P/Bag 461x
Ridgeway 15102
Lusaka
Zambia
a: (011) 260-1-272-394
f: (011) 260-1-224-117

ASIA/PACIFIC

Habitat Australia
P. O. Box 3249
Parramatta NSW 2124
Australia
a: (011) 61-2-680-4433
f: (011) 61-2-689-3111

Fiji National Office
P. O. Box 16154
Suva
Fiji Islands
Phone/Fax: (011) 679-311176

Habitat for Humanity India
17/1 Hosur Road
Richmond Town
Bangalore 560025
India
f: (011) 91-80-225-1468

Indonesia Habitat for Humanity
Kotak Pos 101
Maumre 86111
Flores N. T. T.
Indonesia
f: (011) 62-21-326-044

Habitat New Zealand
P. O. Box 27078
Auckland
New Zealand
a: (011) 649-629-2407
f: (011) 649-535-9542

Pakistan
Contact: Habitat for Humanity International
Americus, GA 31790-3498
(912) 924-6935

Papua New Guinea National Office
P.O. Box 3804
Section 63 Allottment 1
Cassowary Rd
Lae, Morobe Province
Papua New Guinea
Phone/Fax: (011) 675-42-0113

Philippines National Office
P.O. Box 2227
Makati C.P.O.
Metro Manila 1299
Philippines
f: (011) 63-2-894-5229

Solomon Islands
Contact: Habitat for Humanity International
Americus, GA 31709-3498
(912) 924-6935

Sri Lanka Habitat for Humanity
No. 10 Sulaiman Terrace
Colombo 5
Sri Lanka
a: (011) 94-1-588-413
f: (011) 94-1-580-721

CANADA/EUROPE/NEWLY INDEPENDENT STATES

Armenia
Contact: Habitat for Humanity
International
Americus, GA 31709-3498
(912) 924-6935

Habitat Canada
40 Albert St
Waterloo ON N2L 3S2
Canada
a: 519-885-4565
f: 519-885-5225

**Habitat for Humanity
Great Britain**
The Malt House
25-26 Bridge St
Banbury OX16 8PN
England
a: 0295-264240
f: 0295-264230

**Habitat for Humanity in
Northern Ireland at Belfast**
28 Bedford St
Belfast BT2 7FE
N. Ireland
a: (011) 44-1232-243686
f: (011) 44-1232-331878

Habitat for Humanity Hungary
Thokoly ut. 102
4-1146 Budapest
Hungary
Phone/Fax: (011) 361-141-4553

Poland
National Office: Homes of Hope
(Domy Nadziei HFH)
Ul Jaskolcza 9
Gliwice, Katowice, Silesia 44
Poland
f: (011) 48-31-32-4416

THE NETHERLANDS

Habitat for Humanity Nederland
Brugstraat 15
2042 LG Zandvoort
Netherlands
Phone/Fax: (011) 31-3507-30835

LATIN AMERICA/CARIBBEAN

Argentina
Contact: Habitat for Humanity
International
Americus, GA 31709-3498
(912) 924-6935

Habitat Bolivia
Casilla 9573
La Paz
Bolivia
a: (011) 591-281-4982
f: (011) 591-281-4982

Asociacao Habitat Brazil
Rua Tamoios 62, Sala 104
Central Belo Horizonte/Santa
CEP 30120
Brazil
Phone/Fax: (011) 55-31-224-4649

Colombia National Office
Carrera 69 # 53-38
Barrio Normandia
Bogota
Colombia
Phone/Fax: (011) 571-263-5671

Costa Rica
Contact: Habitat for Humanity
International
Americus, GA 31709-3498
(912) 924-6935

Dominican Republic
National Office:
Fundacion Habitat
Republica Dominicana
Apartado #1239
Santo Domingo
Dominican Republic
a: 1-809-549-6934
f: 1-809-547-3501

Habitat El Salvador
Fundacion Techo
Calle Mediterraneo #39
Colonia Jardines de Guadalupe
Antiquo Cuscatlan, La Libertad
El Salvador
Phone/Fax: (011) 503-2223-57-49

Fundacion Habitat Guatemala
8424 NW 56th St. Box Q1011
Miami, FL 33166-3327
f: (011) 50-2-963-5308

Habitat for Humanity Guyana
Contact: Habitat for Humanity
International
Americus, GA 31709-3498
(912) 924-6935, ext. 225

Haiti
Contact: Habitat for Humanity
International
Americus, GA 31709-3498
(912) 924-6935

Habitat Honduras
Apartado 2887
San Pedro Sula
Honduras
Phone/Fax: (011) 504-52-47-42

Habitat Jamaica
28 Upper Waterloo Rd
Kingston 10
Jamaica
a: (809) 926-6568
f: (809) 960-3466

Mexico AC, Habitat para la Humanidad
Mar Negro #6 Col. Tacuba
Deleg. Miguel Hidalgo
Mexico DF C. P. 11410
Mexico
Phone/Fax: (011) 525-527-2684

Habitat Nicaragua
Apartado Postal 2236
Managua
Nicaragua
a: (011) 505-266-6584
f: (011) 505-266-6588

Peru Comite Nacional
Habitat para la Humanidad
Casilla 187
Juliaca
Peru
Phone/Fax: (011) 51-54-351-602

PROSPECTIVE NEW COUNTRIES

Republic of Korea
Zimbabwe
Contact: Habitat for Humanity
Americus, GA 31709-3448
(912) 924-6935, ext. 297

NORTH AMERICAN
NATIONAL/REGIONAL CENTERS

Susan Hancock Sewell, Director
U. S. Affiliates
121 Habitat Street
Americus, GA 31709-3498
(912) 924-6935
f: (912) 924-0577

AREA 1

Barbara Yates, Director
P.O. Box 2322
Acton, MA 01720
(508) 486-9667

Habitat Northeast
Connecticut
Maine
Massachusetts
New Hampshire
New York
Rhode Island
Vermont

Brenda Mleziva, Director
P.O. Box 2322
Acton, MA 01720

(508) 486-4421
f: (508) 486-4678

Habitat East
District of Columbia
Maryland
Virginia
West Virginia

Claire Martindale, Director
P.O. Box 1403
Harrisonburg, VA 22801
(703) 564-0556
f: (703) 564-0650

Habitat Mid-Atlantic
Delaware
New Jersey
Pennsylvania

Robert Warner, Director
P.O. Box 4984
Lancaster, PA 17604-4984
(717) 399-9592
f: (717) 399-9598

AREA 2

Sandra Graham, Director
P.O. Box 16714
Greenville, SC 29606-7714
(803) 235-9887
f: (803) 242-2434

Habitat South Central
Tennessee
Kentucky

Sara Coppler, Director
248 East Short Street
Lexington, KY 40507
(606) 233-7614
f: (606) 233-7806

Habitat Southeast
Florida
Georgia

Dick Weber, Director
226 N. Laura St
Jacksonville, FL 32202-3502
(904) 353-1366
f: (904) 353-1544

Habitat South Atlantic
North Carolina
South Carolina

Gib Edson, Director
P.O. Box 1712
Easley, SC 29640
(803) 855-1102
f: (803) 850-0029

AREA 3

Joe Gatlin, Director
P.O. Box 3005
Waco, TX 76707
(817) 754-4673

Habitat Heartland
Arkansas
Kansas
Missouri
Nebraska

Mark Lassman-Eul, Director
P.O. Box 8955
Springfield, MO 65801-8955
(417) 831-0982
f: (417) 831-0403

Habitat South
Alabama
Louisiana
Mississippi

Bob Yarbrough, Director
P.O. Box 4918
Jackson, MS 39296
(601) 355-4516
f: (601) 355-4928

Habitat Southwest
Oklahoma
Texas

Keith Branson, Director
P.O. Box 3005
Waco, TX 76707
(817) 754-4673
f: (817) 756-3314

AREA 4

Les Alford, Director
1005 NW Galveston
Bend, OR 97701
(503) 388-4583

Habitat Northwest
Alaska
Idaho
Montana
Oregon
Washington

Deanne Everton, Director
1005 NW Galveston
Bend, OR 97701
(503) 383-4637
f: (503) 383-4638

Habitat West
Arizona
California
Hawaii
Nevada

Patricia St. Onge, Director
534 22nd St., Ste. 209
Oakland, CA 94612
(510) 286-8960
f: (510) 286-8969

Habitat Rocky Mountain
Colorado
New Mexico
Utah
Wyoming

Ray Finney, Director
1331 East 31st Ave.
Denver, CO 80205
(303) 296-0978
f: (303) 295-2215

AREA 5

Bill Ward, Director
1920 S. Laflin
Chicago, IL 60608
(708) 904-4553
f: (708) 904-4773

Habitat Mideast
Indiana
Ohio

Margaret Jorgensen, Director
3130 Mayfield Rd., Ste. 310E
Cleveland, OH 44118
(216) 321-0800
f: (216) 321-0650

Habitat Midwest
Illinois
Michigan
Wisconsin

Robert Hall, Director
1920 S. Laflin
Chicago, IL 60608
(312) 243-6448
f: (312) 243-9632

Habitat Upper Midwest
Iowa
Minnesota
North Dakota
South Dakota

Mark Abraham, Director
P.O. Box 23316
Minneapolis, MN 55423-0316
(612) 866-7873
f: (612) 866-7283

SPECIAL OFFICES

American Indian Initiative
Austin Keith, Director
P.O. Box 90
Eagle Butte, SD 57625
(605) 964-8530
f: (605) 964-8531

Church Relations Office
Rick Beech
P.O. Box 1497
Murfreesboro, TN 37133-1497
(615) 893-7990
f: (615) 893-7978

Habitat Washington Office
Thomas L. Jones
1511 K Street NW, Ste. 605
Washington, D. C. 20005
(202) 628-9171
f: (202) 628-9169

Office of Community Investment
Regina Nobles, Director
5446 Richmond Street
Dallas, TX 75206
(214) 826-1742
f: (214) 827-1619

Urban Initiative
Karen Young
P.O. Box 920884
Houston, TX 77292-0884
(713) 802-2618
f: (713) 802-0247

LaFrontera Initiative
Daniel Lopez, Director
1701 N., 8th St., A-18
McAllen, TX 78501
(210) 682-7277
f: (210) 687-9266

Additional Resources

Books and Videos About the Ministry of Habitat for Humanity

The Theology of the Hammer—The important biblical teachings and principles that have guided Habitat for Humanity from the inception of the ministry, brought to life in action. By Millard Fuller. (1994)

The Excitement is Building—How Habitat for Humanity continued to grow while putting roofs over heads, and hope in hearts. By Millard and Linda Fuller. (1990)

No More Shacks!—The vision and incredible goal of Habitat for Humanity to rid the world of shacks and replace them with simple, decent places to live. By Millard Fuller with Diane Scott. (1986)

Love in the Mortar Joints—The story of Habitat for Humanity's first four years of growth; the launching of sixteen projects in North America, Africa, and Central America. By Millard Fuller and Diane Scott. (1980)

Bokotola—Habitat's beginnings as a housing ministry in Mbandaka, Zaire, and the vision of providing decent housing for God's people in need all over the world. By Millard Fuller. (1977)

Videos and Audiocassettes

"The Theology of the Hammer"—The Spoken Word (audiocassettes)—Two 90-minute audiocassettes, recorded by Millard Fuller, reading from his book of the same name. (1994)

"Sermons of Love"—Video tells about Habitat affiliates and churches in partnership with each other and God's people in need.

"Building New Lives"—A brief history of Habitat for Humanity with an overview of the work in the United States and around the world.

"Building on Common Ground"—The exciting account of the 1992 Jimmy Carter Work Project in Washington, D. C.

"Building Tomorrow"—Introduction to Habitat's Campus Chapters program for student groups.

"Circle of Hope"—Inspiring and colorful visual account of Habitat's work at the Cheyenne River Sioux Indian Reservation in Eagle Butte, South Dakota.

"The Excitement is Building"—The story of Habitat for Humanity up through the 1988 Jimmy Carter Work Project and the Twelfth Anniversary Celebration in Atlanta.

"Miracle on the Border"—The heartwarming account of Habitat's historic 1990 blitz build which spanned the border, with houses being built in San Diego and Tijuana, Mexico.

Other books, videos, and audiocassettes about the ministry of Habitat for Humanity are available by writing:

> Habitat for Humanity International
> 121 Habitat Street
> Americus, GA 31709-3498.

Glossary of Habitat Terms

Adopt-a-Home—Churches or other organizations that adopt a home provide all the funding and labor needed for construction of a specific house. A church or organization can adopt a home on its own, or two or more groups can form a partnership to fund and construct a house. Groups working in partnership may team up to work on an entire project together.

Affiliates—Local independent, nonprofit organizations responsible for directing Habitat for Humanity house-building work in their communities. They are a foundation of Habitat's grass-roots approach, with all decisions made at the local level, within the context of a signed agreement (covenant) with Habitat for Humanity International. Affiliates are primarily responsible for their own fund-raising and are expected to tithe 10 percent of their undesignated income to Habitat headquarters for work in developing countries.

Biblical economics—Also known as the "economics of Jesus," is summarized as follows: No profit added and no interest charged on Habitat houses, in compliance with the biblical admonition to charge no interest to the poor (Ex. 22:25 and elsewhere in Scripture). Furthermore, such "economics" assure a multiplication of small resources into enough to get the job done if all that is available is offered for use and if God is called upon to increase the resources. The model for such multiplication is Jesus' feeding of the multitude with five loaves of bread and two fishes. "Biblical economics" also embrace the concept that every human life is priceless, no matter how insignificant it may seem.

Blitz build—A house-raising project in which a Habitat for Humanity house or houses are built within a very concentrated period of time—usually one week or less, and typically by volunteers from a church, association, or business, or a combination of such sponsoring organizations.

Covenant—The basic document that defines the relationship between Habitat for Humanity International and local affiliates (see Appendix One).

Fund for Humanity—A local, revolving fund that exists at every Habitat affiliate, consisting of funds from Habitat house payments, contributions from individuals and organizations, and income from fund-raising projects. Money in this "fund" is recycled promptly to build more houses.

"Infectious habititis"—A humorous term used to describe the "infectious enthusiasm" of someone who is deeply committed to the ministry of Habitat for Humanity.

"Love in the mortar joints"—A basic philosophy of Habitat for Humanity which mandates that people-building and love relationships with the homeowner families and with all parties in the building partnership are equally important to the actual building of the houses.

A simple, decent place to live.—The term to describe a Habitat house and the overall approach to its construction. It means Habitat builds houses that are basic in design and construction and without frills—homes that are built to last and withstand the batterings of inclement and even violent weather.

Sweat equity—This is the unpaid labor invested by homeowner partners in working on their own houses and those of others. These non-paid work hours are a requirement for Habitat homeownership. Sweat equity reduces the monetary cost of building a house and increases the personal stake of each family member in their home.

"Theology of the hammer"—This simply means that people will agree on the use of the hammer as an instrument to manifest God's love. We may disagree on all sorts of other things—baptism, communion, what night to have prayer meetings, and how the preacher should dress—but we can agree on the imperative of the gospel to serve others in the name of the Lord. This simple theology also embraces the idea that true religion is more than singing hymns and talking about faith; it also includes action.

Notes

Chapter 1

No notes.

Chapter 2

No notes.

Chapter 3

1. "Building on Faith Project" involved the participation and house-building of ten affiliates, all visited by Millard Fuller in 1995. They were North Alabama HFH, Huntsville, AL; Greater Lynchburg HFH, Lynchburg, VA; Central Oklahoma HFH, Oklahoma City, OK; Twin Cities HFH, Minneapolis, MN; HFH of Greater Indianapolis, Indianapolis, IN; Central South Carolina HFH, Columbia, SC; Montgomery HFH, Montgomery, AL; Greenville County HFH, Greenville, SC; Thermal Belt HFH, Tryon, NC; Fresno HFH, Fresno, CA.

Chapter 4

1. "Hands Across The Prairie," and "Habitat Vision Changes Reservation Reality," by Karen Free, *Habitat World*, October 1994.

Chapter 5

1. "House Raisings Help Root Out Crime," by Bob Yarbrough, *Habitat World*, December 1994.
2. "Changing Lives: Habitat Makes a Difference," by Terri Franklin, *Habitat World*, December 1994.
3. Ibid.
4. Ibid.
5. "Catch a Rising Star," by Terri Franklin, *Habitat World*, December 1994.

Chapter 6

No notes.

Chapter 7

1. Under the laws of many states, an individual must be at least eighteen, nineteen, or twenty-one years of age in order to serve as a director of a nonprofit corporation. Therefore, any nonprofit organization should check with its attorney before electing anyone under the age of twenty-one to its board of directors in order to ensure that it is in compliance with the laws of its state of incorporation.
2. "Benchmarks," by Milana McLead, *Habitat World*, December 1994.
3. "Ghana Gives Visitors a Lesson in Need," by Robin Chenoweth, *Habitat World*, February 1993, excerpted with permission from the *Columbus* [Ohio] *Dispatch*.
4. Address for Jack and Lois Wolters, coordinators of the RV Gypsies: Route 1, Box 442, Columbus, North Carolina, 28722.
5. "The Work Changed My Life . . . My Heart, Spirit, and Soul," excerpt by Tom Schmidt, *Habitat World*, June 1993.
6. "The Work Changed My Life . . . My Heart, Spirit, and Soul," excerpt by Willie Wilkerson, *Habitat World*, June 1993.

Chapter 8

1. "Building Houses and Hope in Northern Ireland," by Jane McCarthy, *Habitat World*, October 1994.
2. "Sing-Singing the Night Away," by Nancy Cardwell, *Habitat World*, February 1994.
3. "Building New Traditions," by Donna Minich, *Habitat World*, December 1994.
4. "Construction Goes Cross-Country in Canada," by Shayla Stevens, *Habitat World*, October 1994.
5. "Overcoming Obstacles Overseas," by Tilly Grey, *Habitat World*, December 1994.
6. "Bless the Beasts and the Homeowners," by Terri Franklin, *Habitat World*, October 1994.

Chapter 9

1. "Big Business, Big Hearts," by Tilly Grey, *Habitat World*, October 1994.

Chapter 10

No notes.

Maps

1. Habitat for Humanity Around the World
2. Habitat for Humanity Affiliates in the United States
3. Millard Fuller's International Travels for Habitat for Humanity

Habitat for Humanity Around the World

(Status as of May 1995)

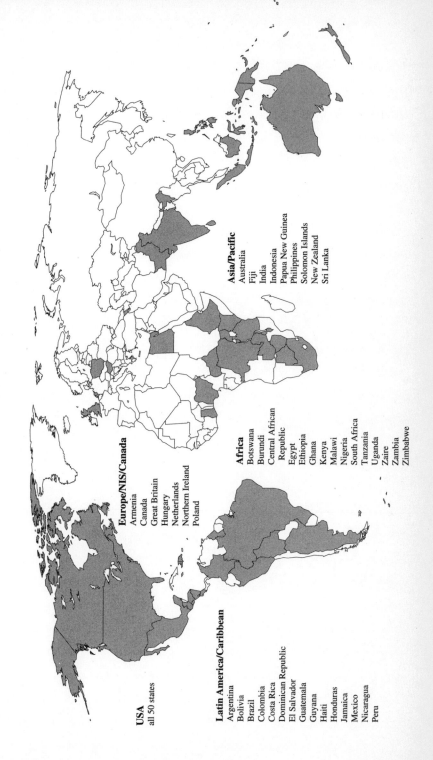

USA
all 50 states

Latin America/Caribbean
Argentina
Bolivia
Brazil
Colombia
Costa Rica
Dominican Republic
El Salvador
Guatemala
Guyana
Haiti
Honduras
Jamaica
Mexico
Nicaragua
Peru

Europe/NIS/Canada
Armenia
Canada
Great Britain
Hungary
Netherlands
Northern Ireland
Poland

Africa
Botswana
Burundi
Central African Republic
Egypt
Ethiopia
Ghana
Kenya
Malawi
Nigeria
South Africa
Tanzania
Uganda
Zaire
Zambia
Zimbabwe

Asia/Pacific
Australia
Fiji
India
Indonesia
Papua New Guinea
Philippines
Solomon Islands
New Zealand
Sri Lanka

Habitat for Humanity Affiliates in the United States

As of May 1995, there were 1,136 Habitat for Humanity affiliates in communities across the United States. At present we add affiliates at a rate of ten to fifteen each month.

233

Millard Fuller's International Travels for Habitat for Humanity

January 1993 through July 1995

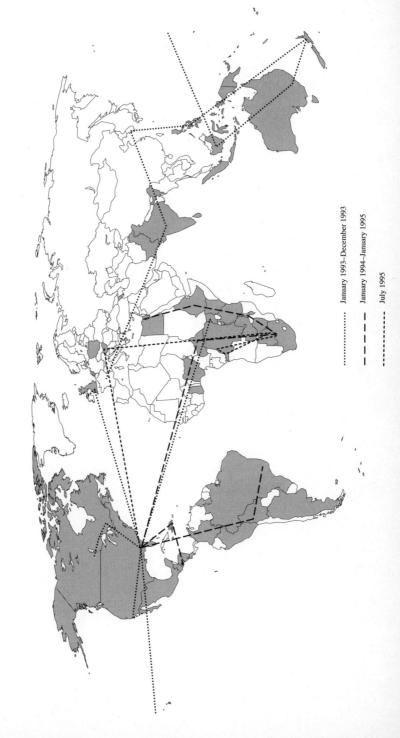

.... January 1993–December 1993

– – – – January 1994–January 1995

- - - - July 1995